why throw it away?

JEN GREEN

SHOOTING STAR PRESS

CONTENTS

INTRODUCTION

This book will show you how to make your own collection of masks and crazy faces, crazy animals, mad machines and fantastic aliens and spaceships. Each of the projects is explained in easy stages. There are also more ideas about how you can adapt the models, bringing in your own imagination.

Other ideas

All the projects shown here can be made with everyday junk that is usually thrown away. Each project includes a list of junk items used to make the model. Collect your materials together before you begin. If you haven't got one of the items suggested, you may have something else that will do just as well.

Your junk box

Start your own collection of junk now. Save any materials that might come in handy, and ask your family to pass junk on to you rather than throw it away. Make sure your materials are clean before you store them in plastic bags or cardboard boxes. For more ideas about collecting junk, see pages 29, 55, 81, or 107.

5

CRAZY CLOWN

This happy clown face is built on a paper plate base. You can decorate the plate with different materials to create other faces, either human or animal.

1 This paper plate mask will fit over your face. To make eyeholes, look in a mirror and measure the distance between your eyes with a ruler. Mark your measurements on the mask and pierce the eyeholes. Cut shapes for the eyes from colored paper. Cut out the pupils. Tape on the eyes and a plastic lid for the nose.

2 Cut out and tape on a sad or smiling paper mouth. The clown's hat is a small tinfoil tray. Cut out a small paper flower for the hat, and tape it on. Tape or glue on strands of yarn for the hair.

3 Attach the hat to the clown's head with tape or a paper clip. Make a small hole on each side of the face, under the hair. Measure a piece of string or elastic to go around the back of your head. Thread it through the holes, and knot the ends.

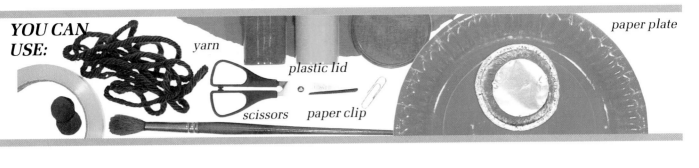

YOU CAN USE:

yarn

plastic lid

scissors

paper clip

paper plate

If you haven't got a paper plate, make a cardboard circle instead. Draw around a circular object on cardboard and cut out the shape with scissors.

A paper plate can form the basis of many other masks. The junk items you have collected may suggest a character to you. You could try a chef, pirate, burglar, bandit, police officer, a cowboy or cowgirl.

GINGER CAT

Paper bags make good masks that fit right over your head. The design shown here can easily be adapted to make many animal characters.

STEP BY STEP

1 Make sure the bag fits over your head before you begin. **Do not use plastic bags; they are too dangerous.** Cut two diagonal slits into the bottom of the bag. **2** Glue on

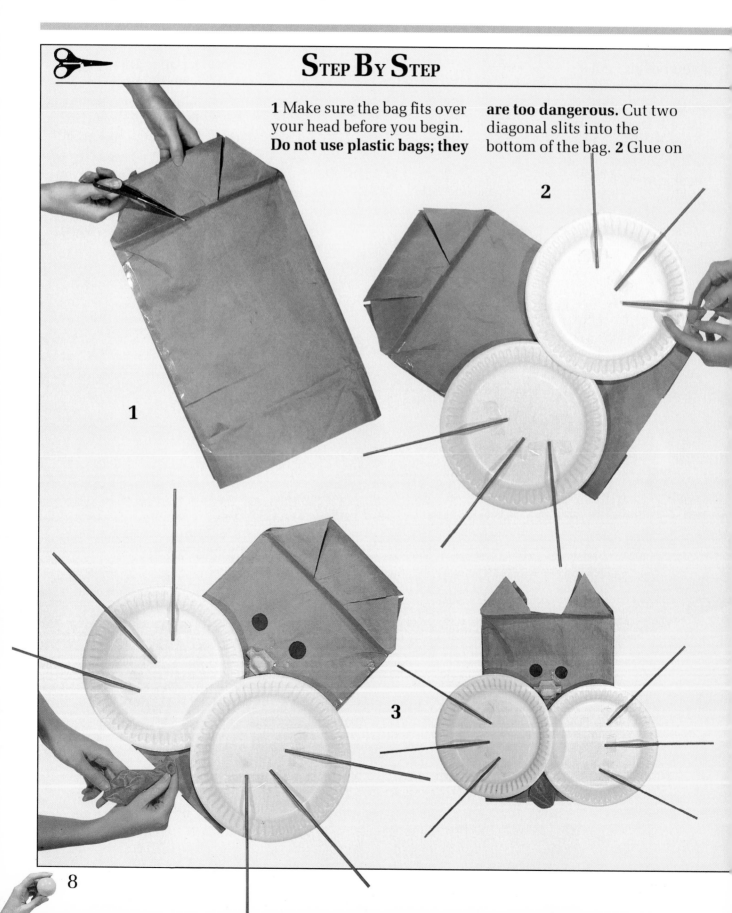

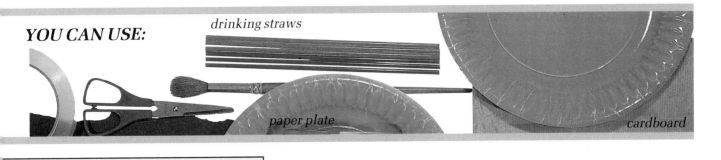

two paper plates for the cat's cheeks. You could also attach them with double-sided tape (see page 28). Tape on drinking straws for the cat's whiskers.

3 Cut a section from an egg carton to make the nose. Tape on a red balloon for the tongue. Mark eyeholes as you did for the clown mask. Cut small black paper circles for eyes, and glue them on the points you've marked. Pierce through the eyes with scissors when the glue is dry.

Decorate your bag mask with thick poster paint. You could make your cat a ginger tom, or a tabby cat with brown and black stripes.

This mask can be adapted to make a dog, a squirrel, and many other animals. You could try a tiger, or a lion with a mane of woolly strands.

You could use a cork, bottle top, or plastic cup to make the nose. You could use pipe cleaners to make whiskers, and cardboard for the nose.

9

ALIEN FROM OUTER SPACE

This scary alien has a single eye in the middle of its forehead, and jagged teeth.
You can adapt this design to make a robot and other space monsters.

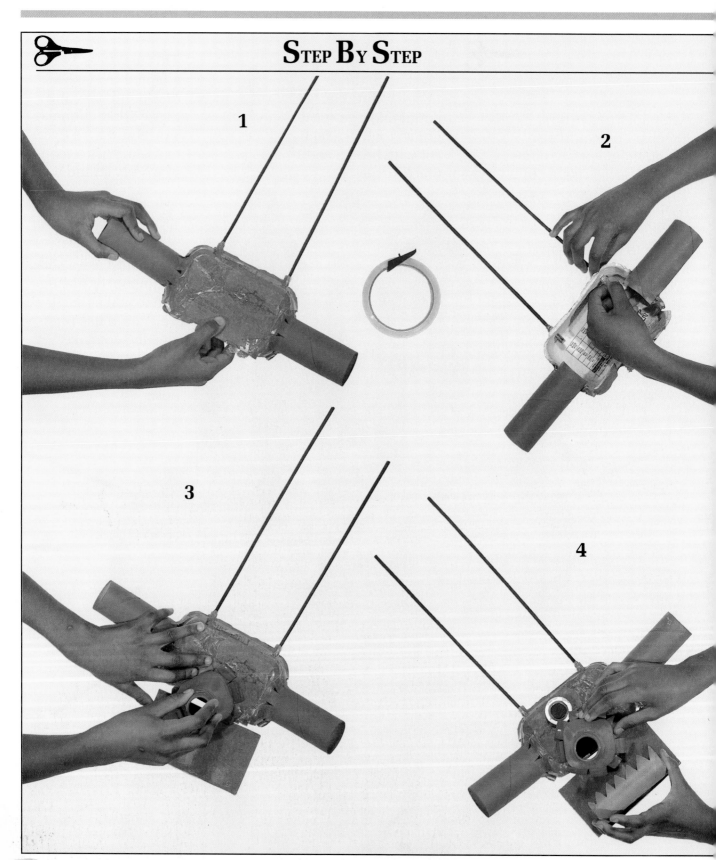

YOU CAN USE:

cardboard packet

garden sticks

plastic bottle
three toilet
paper tubes

egg carton

1 Cut an egg carton in half to form the alien's head. The ears are two toilet paper tubes. Cut a series of slits into one end of both tubes. Splay the cut ends flat, and tape them to the sides of the egg carton (see Practical Tips on page 28). Pierce two holes in the top of the head. Push through two sticks to make antennae. 2 Wind tape around the sticks on either side of the egg carton, to anchor the antennae in place. 3 Tape a cardboard box onto the egg carton to make the alien's jaw. For the nose, cut off the top of a plastic bottle. Cut flaps into the end and fold them over, as you did for the ears. Tape on the nose. 4 Cut another cardboard tube in half and cut out a line of jagged teeth. Tape the teeth onto the jaw. Tape on the lid of a plastic bottle to make the eye. Mark and pierce eyeholes as you have before. Make holes in the sides of the mask, and thread through string or elastic to fit around your head.

The basis of this mask can be a cardboard box of any size, an egg box or even a paper plate.

Your junk box may have other ingredients that can be used to make different alien faces. Plastic cups or even rubber gloves could be used for ears. Straws could be used for antennae. Some aliens do not have eyes, nose, and mouth arranged on the face in the same positions as we humans do.

WACKY SPECS

These zany glasses are easy to make and fun to wear. Their brightly colored eyeballs bounce crazily, and pop out on long, springy stalks.

STEP BY STEP

1 The lenses of your wacky specs are two toilet paper tubes. Cut two rectangles of colored paper to make eyelashes. Fringe the paper with scissors, cutting a series of slits down one side as shown. Roll the fringe around a pencil or around your scissors, to make the eyelashes curl up.

2 Tape the eyelashes around one end of both tubes. The eyeballs are two Ping Pong balls. Cut two long, narrow strips down the side of a plastic bottle to make stalks for the eyeballs. The strips should fit inside the tubes. Crease the strips into accordion folds. Tape an eyeball to one end of each.

3 Push the stalks through the tubes. Secure them inside the tubes with tape. Push the eyeballs into the tubes and make sure they pop out freely!

4 Cut a strip of thick cardboard to make the bridge between the lenses. Tape on the bridge. Cut long strips from cardboard or from the lid of an egg carton, to make earpieces, curved to fit around your ears.

5 Tape them on as shown.

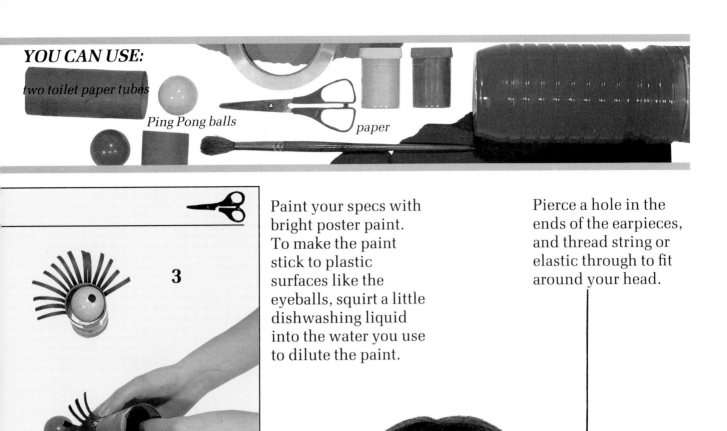

YOU CAN USE:

two toilet paper tubes

Ping Pong balls

paper

3

Paint your specs with bright poster paint. To make the paint stick to plastic surfaces like the eyeballs, squirt a little dishwashing liquid into the water you use to dilute the paint.

Pierce a hole in the ends of the earpieces, and thread string or elastic through to fit around your head.

ARROW HEADBAND

Horrify your friends and family with this lifelike arrow headgear and its blood-soaked bandage. It can easily be made into a sword or dagger wound.

STEP BY STEP

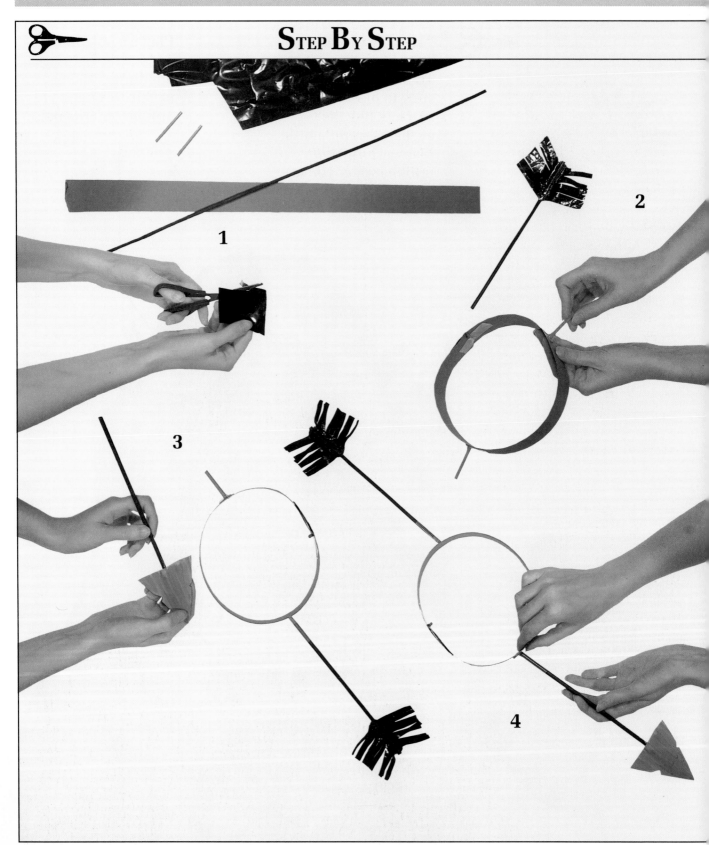

YOU CAN USE:

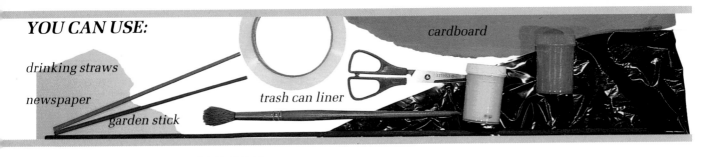

drinking straws

newspaper

garden stick

trash can liner

cardboard

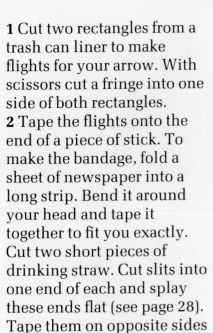

1 Cut two rectangles from a trash can liner to make flights for your arrow. With scissors cut a fringe into one side of both rectangles.
2 Tape the flights onto the end of a piece of stick. To make the bandage, fold a sheet of newspaper into a long strip. Bend it around your head and tape it together to fit you exactly. Cut two short pieces of drinking straw. Cut slits into one end of each and splay these ends flat (see page 28). Tape them on opposite sides of the bandage. The flighted end of the arrow fits into one straw. To make the point of

the arrow, cut out two triangles of cardboard. Glue them together on either side of another piece of stick.
3 Cut small nicks into the arrowhead to make it look really authentic. 4 Slot the stick into the other straw.

Paint the bandage white with fine black lines so it looks as if it has been wound around your head. Paint red blood dripping from the wounds where the arrow has pierced through your head!

You may want to moan and groan while you are wearing this headgear, to make it even more convincing!

15

STEAMSHIP HAT

This wonderful hat will create a stir at parties and get-togethers. It is light and made to fit your head exactly.

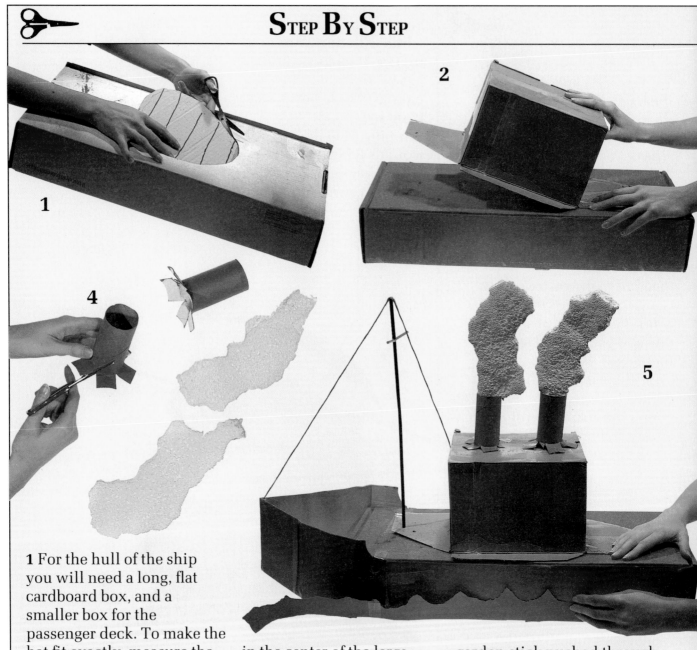

1 For the hull of the ship you will need a long, flat cardboard box, and a smaller box for the passenger deck. To make the hat fit exactly, measure the dimensions of your head, or get someone to draw around it on a piece of paper. Mark your measurements on the bottom of the flat box. Then cut out a hole for your head. Turn the box over. **2** Open the smaller box and place it in the center of the large one. Trim the flaps of the small box and tape them to the large one. **3** Cut a long cardboard strip to make the prow (front) of the boat. Fold the strip in half and tape the ends to the hull. The mast of the ship is a garden stick pushed through a small hole in the top of the flat box. Cut a straw in half to make a crosspiece for the mast. Pierce a small hole through the straw so that you can thread it onto the mast. Measure and cut a length of string for the

two toilet paper tubes

styrofoam or cardboard   garden stick   string

large and small cardboard boxes

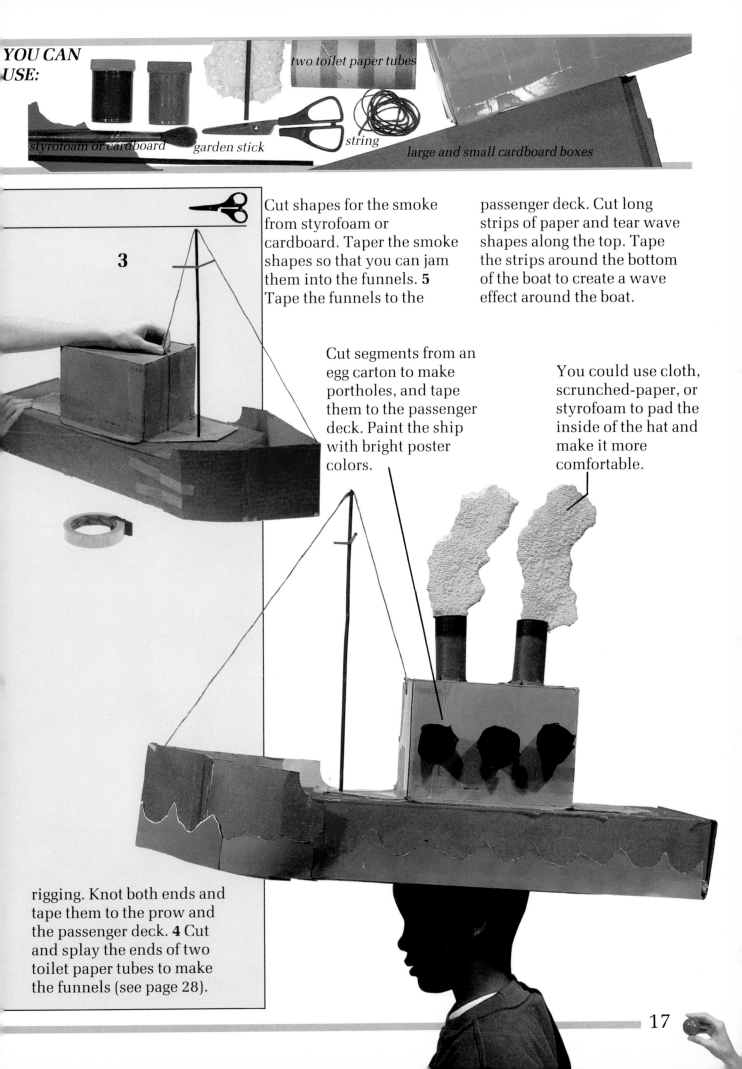

3

Cut shapes for the smoke from styrofoam or cardboard. Taper the smoke shapes so that you can jam them into the funnels. **5** Tape the funnels to the passenger deck. Cut long strips of paper and tear wave shapes along the top. Tape the strips around the bottom of the boat to create a wave effect around the boat.

Cut segments from an egg carton to make portholes, and tape them to the passenger deck. Paint the ship with bright poster colors.

You could use cloth, scrunched-paper, or styrofoam to pad the inside of the hat and make it more comfortable.

rigging. Knot both ends and tape them to the prow and the passenger deck. **4** Cut and splay the ends of two toilet paper tubes to make the funnels (see page 28).

ANIMAL PARTY MASKS

Half-masks were traditionally worn at masquerades or masked balls. These animal faces are made using the half-mask pattern on page 31.

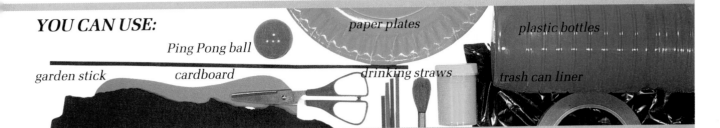

To make the mouse:

1 Trace the mask on page 31 onto cardboard, and cut it out. Cut off the neck of a plastic bottle for the nose. Cut a slit in the back of it. **2** Slot the mask into the slit. Cut and splay the ends of six straws, and tape them to the nose for whiskers. Cut and tape on paper teeth. Add a Ping Pong ball nose. **3** Tape a cane to the nose, to hold the mask to your face.

To make the elephant:

1 Tape two paper plates to the mask for the elephant's ears. Cut off any cardboard that may cover the mask's eyeholes. **2** Cut off the top of a small plastic bottle for the trunk. Cut slits into the sides, and slot the trunk onto the mask. Tape on a stick.

To make the crow:

1 Cut out the feathers from a plastic trash can liner, using the pattern on page 31. Tape straws to the back of the feathers. **2** Cut a long triangle of cardboard for the beak, and cut nostrils. Fold the beak in half. Cut a short slit into it and fold the ends over. **3** Tape the ends to the mask. Tape on a stick.

Your junk box may contain bits and pieces that suggest other animals for you to try.

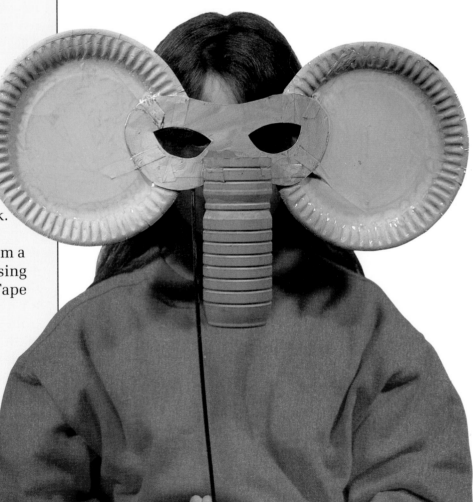

19

ASTRONAUT'S HELMET

This mask, a must for all space games, is based on a shell made of papier mâché. It is a vital piece of equipment when visiting alien worlds.

You could cut zigzag shapes from paper and glue them on to decorate the visor.

You could add a stars and stripes flag, painted on or made with pieces of straw.

Measure and pierce two small eyeholes in the mask with scissors. Alternatively, you could make the visor from transparent plastic so that you can see out more easily.

1 To make papier mâché, mix flour and a little water in a bowl, until you have a thick paste. Tear a newspaper into strips. Blow up a balloon and stand it in another bowl. Dip a strip in the paste, run it through your fingers to remove excess paste, and lay it on the balloon. Repeat this until the top half of the balloon is covered with at least three layers of newspaper. Leave it to dry overnight. Burst the balloon. **2** Trim the bottom of the papier mâché shape flat with scissors. Draw on the shape of the visor, and cut it out with scissors. **3** Cut two segments from an egg carton to make earpieces, and tape them on the sides of the helmet. **4** Cut out a circular piece of trash can liner to make the visor, and tape it inside the helmet. **5** The astronauts's eyes are two Ping Pong balls, and the nose is a cork. Cut eyebrows from an egg carton and tape all these features to the visor. Splay one end of a drinking straw, and tape it to the top of the helmet to make a radio receiver. Pierce a hole through the straw, cut another straw in half and push it through the hole, to form a crosspiece.

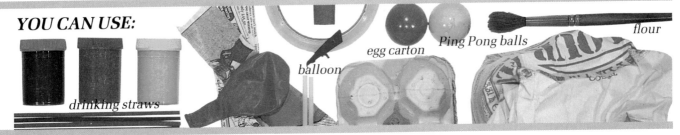

STEP BY STEP

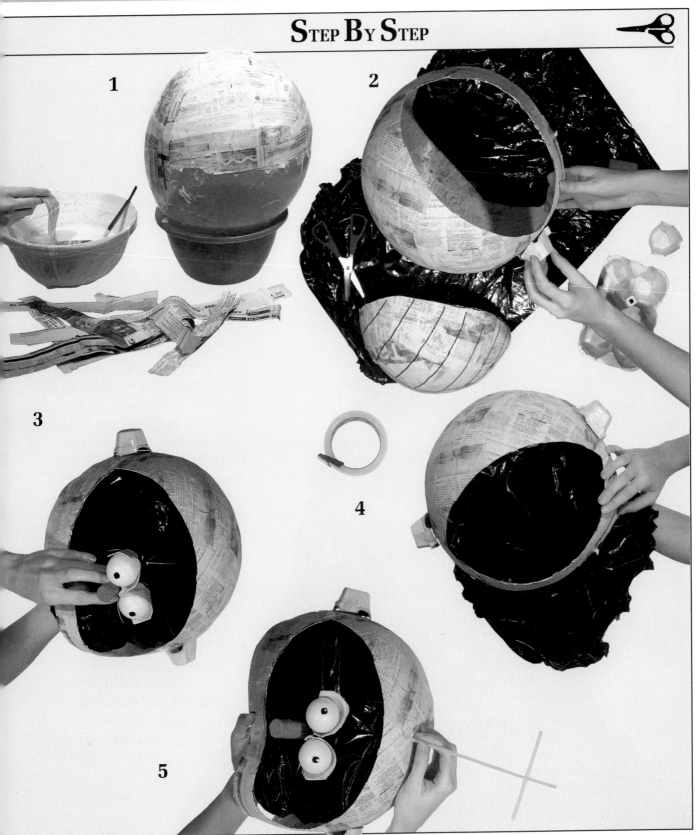

1

2

3

4

5

Viking Helmet

The Vikings were a warlike people from Scandinavia who pillaged and plundered the coasts of Europe in their longboats in the 9th and 10th centuries.

You could make the hair and moustache from strands of yarn or even string.

Segments cut from a chocolate box tray could be used to decorate the helmet.

1 To make the papier mâché shell see pages 20-1. Blow up a balloon and stand it nozzle upward in a bowl. Dip the paper strips into the paste, and lay them on the balloon. Continue until the end of the balloon is covered with at least three layers of newspaper. 2 Leave it to dry overnight, then pop the balloon. Trim the rim with scissors. Make two horns for the helmet from paper cones (see page 28). Cut slits into the bottom of the cones, to create a series of flaps. 3 Tape the horns by the flaps onto the papier mâché shell. Cut a rectangle of cardboard to make your noseguard. Cut a strip of colored paper to make the hair. Fringe the paper with scissors. 4 Tape the fringe inside the helmet. 5 Cut a smaller strip of paper to make a moustache. Fringe both sides of the strip towards the middle. Roll it up and tape it to the bottom of the noseguard. Tape the noseguard inside the front of the helmet. Cut segments from an egg carton to decorate the front of the helmet, and tape them on.

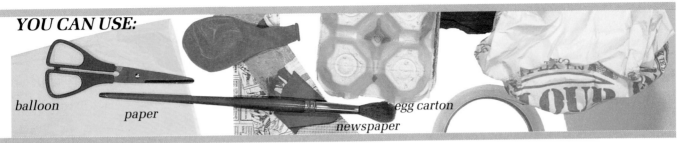

balloon

paper

newspaper

egg carton

STEP BY STEP

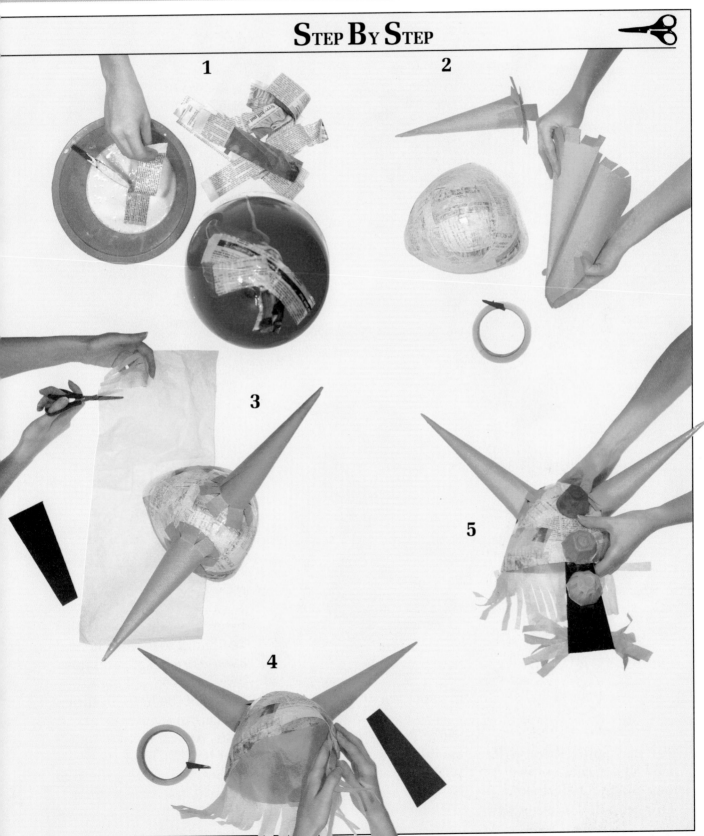

1

2

3

4

5

JESTER'S HAT

In medieval times, jesters were professional clowns hired to entertain lords and ladies at court. You will need a good supply of jokes when you wear this mask!

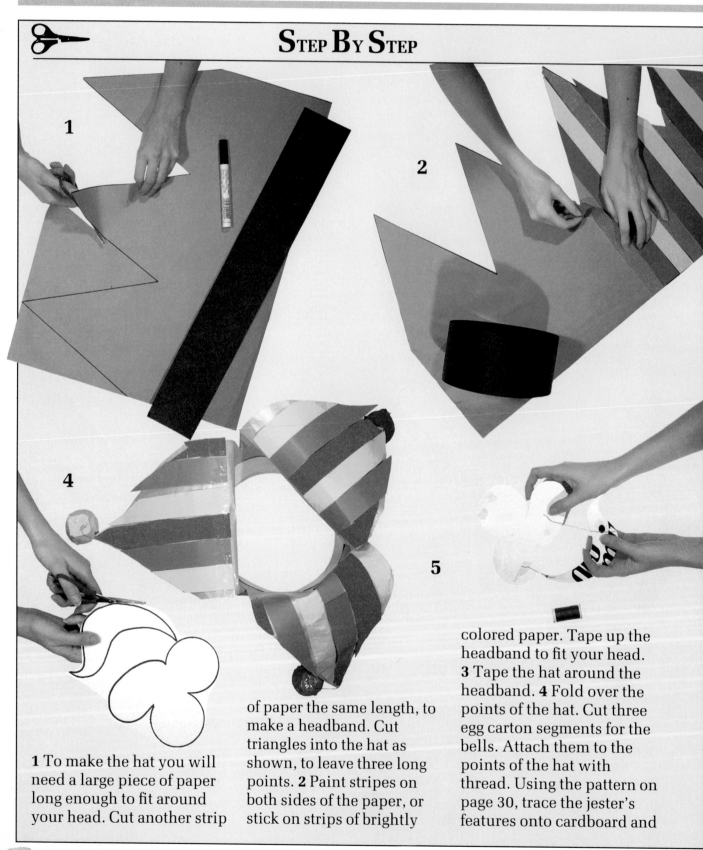

STEP BY STEP

1 To make the hat you will need a large piece of paper long enough to fit around your head. Cut another strip of paper the same length, to make a headband. Cut triangles into the hat as shown, to leave three long points. **2** Paint stripes on both sides of the paper, or stick on strips of brightly colored paper. Tape up the headband to fit your head. **3** Tape the hat around the headband. **4** Fold over the points of the hat. Cut three egg carton segments for the bells. Attach them to the points of the hat with thread. Using the pattern on page 30, trace the jester's features onto cardboard and

3

You could wear the hat without the jester's features, if you prefer. It could be fun to use face paints to make up your own face to complete the jester look.

You could use Ping Pong balls or scrunched-up balls of paper to make the bells.

6

cut them out. **5** Attach the mouth to the eyes and nose with thread. Paint the eyes, nose and mouth with bright poster colors. **6** Attach the features to the hat using double-sided tape (see page 28). Measure and pierce eye-holes in the mask.

SNAPPING DRAGON

This spectacular mask has a hinged lip which you can raise to reveal a fearsome set of teeth. You can adapt this design to make a dinosaur or a crocodile.

STEP BY STEP

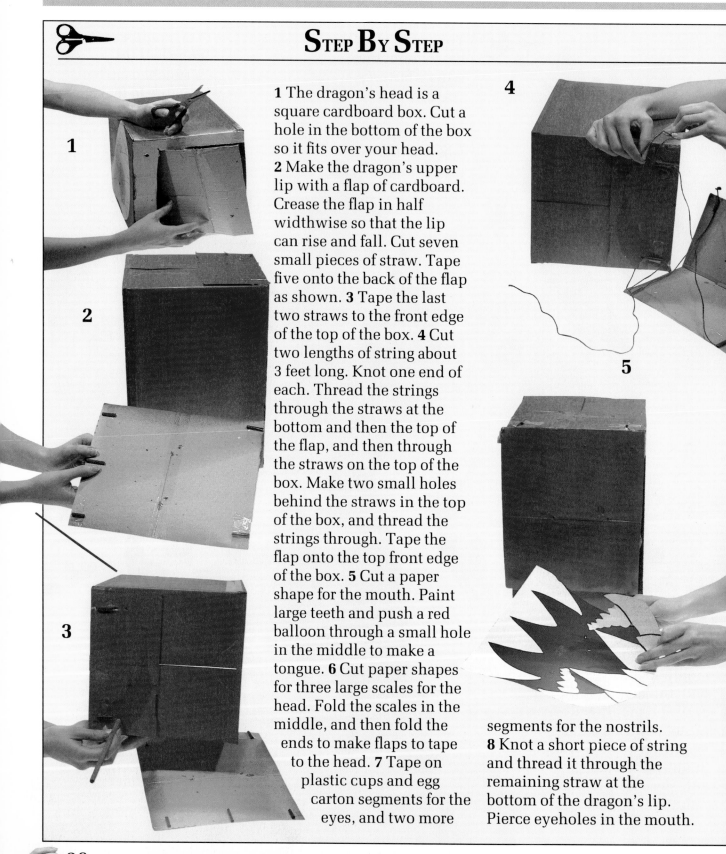

1 The dragon's head is a square cardboard box. Cut a hole in the bottom of the box so it fits over your head. 2 Make the dragon's upper lip with a flap of cardboard. Crease the flap in half widthwise so that the lip can rise and fall. Cut seven small pieces of straw. Tape five onto the back of the flap as shown. 3 Tape the last two straws to the front edge of the top of the box. 4 Cut two lengths of string about 3 feet long. Knot one end of each. Thread the strings through the straws at the bottom and then the top of the flap, and then through the straws on the top of the box. Make two small holes behind the straws in the top of the box, and thread the strings through. Tape the flap onto the top front edge of the box. 5 Cut a paper shape for the mouth. Paint large teeth and push a red balloon through a small hole in the middle to make a tongue. 6 Cut paper shapes for three large scales for the head. Fold the scales in the middle, and then fold the ends to make flaps to tape to the head. 7 Tape on plastic cups and egg carton segments for the eyes, and two more segments for the nostrils.
8 Knot a short piece of string and thread it through the remaining straw at the bottom of the dragon's lip. Pierce eyeholes in the mouth.

6

7

8

When you pull on the two strings inside the box, the dragon's upper lip should lift to reveal its teeth; when you pull the short string, the lip will fall again.

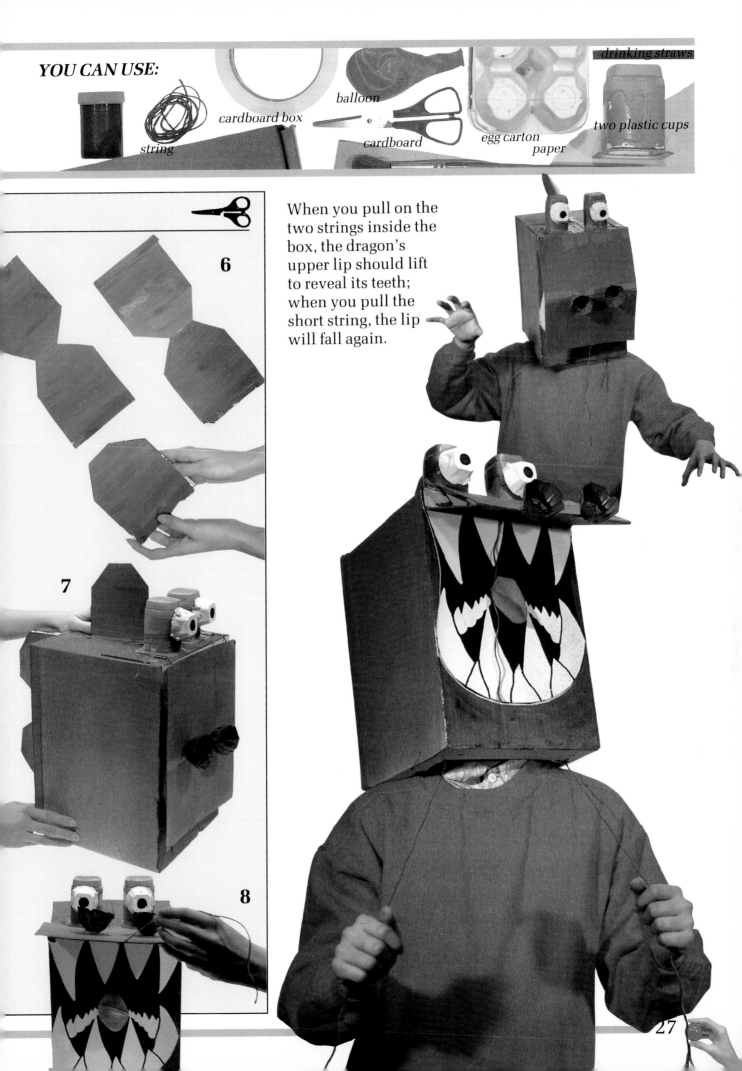

PRACTICAL TIPS

Below are a few practical hints to help you with some of the masks described in this book, and with your craft projects in general.

DOUBLE-SIDED TAPE

Double-sided sticky tape is useful when you don't want tape to show on your models. You can buy rolls of this tape in craft and stationery stores, or you can make your own. Cut a short length of tape and roll it over itself until you can stick one end to the other.

CREATING FLAPS

Use this whenever you need to fasten tube shapes onto your models. Use scissors to cut a number of short slits into one end of the tube. The slits form a series of flaps around the end. Bend the flaps over, and press the tube flat onto the surface of your model. Attach the flaps to the model with glue, tape or even papier mâché.

MAKING A CONE

To make horns for the Viking helmet on pages 22-23, you need to construct paper cones. You will need pieces of paper about 10 inches square. Roll each piece into a cone, pulling the edge of the paper inside the cone to make a fine point. Tape up the point, and tape along the edge of the rolled paper. Trim the bottom edge of the cone flat with scissors. Cut slits into the bottom edge, to create a series of flaps. Bend the

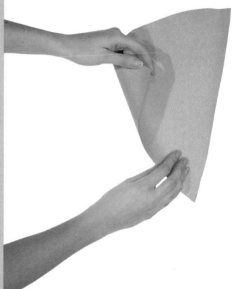

flaps over so that you can tape the cones onto the flat surface of the helmet.

FABRIC: socks, old clothes or sheets, cloth, felt scraps, and yarn.

MORE JUNK IDEAS

Chestnuts, corks, and eggshells can be used to make eyes, ears, or noses for your masks. Rubber gloves, tin cans, or even socks can form the basis of arms and legs.

The materials used most often in this book have been paper, cardboard and plastic packaging. Below are some more suggestions about the kinds of junk that can be used to make and decorate your models.

NATURAL MATERIALS: twigs, leaves, petals, acorns, nuts, pinecones, bark, shells, pebbles, sponge, cork, feathers.

RUBBER: rubber bands, balloons, rubber gloves.

PAPER: newspapers, comics and magazines, postcards and birthday cards, unused wallpaper, tissue.

WOOD: spent matches, garden sticks, clothes pegs, cotton spools, popsicle sticks.

PLASTIC: food containers, candy and snack wrappers, buttons, broken toys.

METAL: soft drink cans, tin-foil, springs, pipe cleaners, coat hangers, paper clips.

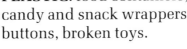

PATTERNS

These patterns will help you with some of the projects in this book.

◀ Use the patterns on page 30 to make the jester's features for pages 24-25.

To use the patterns:
1 Trace the pattern shapes onto tracing paper.
2 Turn the tracing over, and place it on top of paper or cardboard. Scribble over the lines showing through the paper with your pencil. A mirror image of the pattern will appear on the cardboard. **3** If you want the patterns on page 30 to appear the right way round: turn the tracing paper over again, and place it over paper or cardboard.
4 Draw carefully over your image again.

▲ Trace the pattern at the top to make the crow's feathers on pages 18-19.

▶ Use this pattern to make the party masks on pages 18-19. You will find the eyeholes easier to cut out if you push the point of your pencil through the middle of the shape first, to make a hole for your scissors.

CRAZY ANIMAL HEADS

These colorful animal heads are all made from odds and ends of junk stuck onto a cardboard base such as a paper plate. You can use the same methods with different ingredients to make your own animal heads.

STEP BY STEP

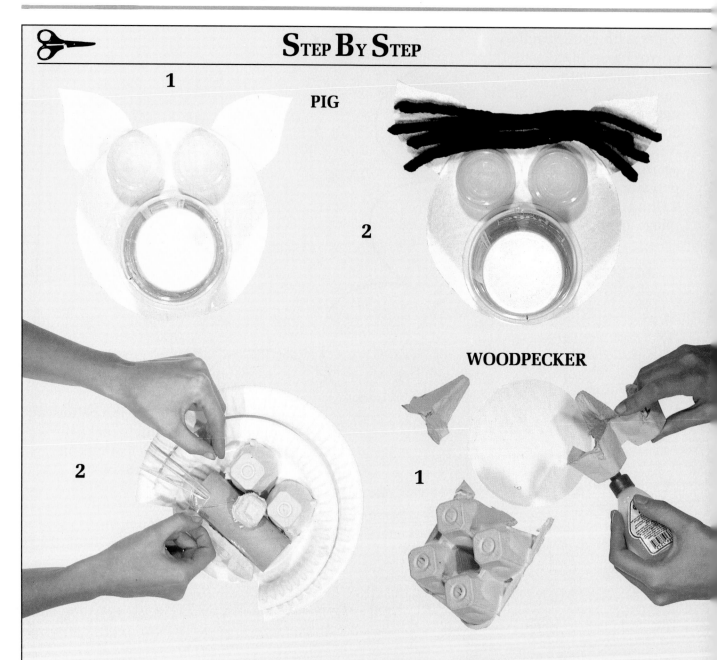

1

PIG

2

WOODPECKER

2

1

To make the pig:
1 You will need two bottle tops for eyes, a plastic cup for the nose, yarn, ear shapes cut from cardboard, and a cardboard circle for the head. You could make the circle by cutting the rim off a paper plate. **2** Tape or

glue on the bottle tops to make the eyes and the cup for the nose. Glue on yarn for the hair.

To make the lion:
1 You will need two sections cut from an egg carton for the eyes, a toilet paper tube for the muzzle,

toothpicks for whiskers, and two paper plates with part of the rims cut away. **2** Glue one plate inside the other to make the mane. Cut the toilet tube in half to make a muzzle. Add egg carton eyes, nose and teeth. Lastly, tape on toothpick whiskers.

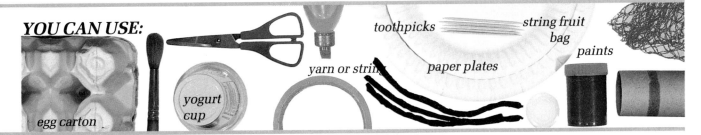

toothpicks

string fruit bag

yarn or string

paper plates

paints

yogurt cup

egg carton

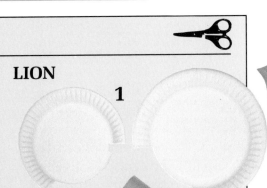

LION

1

2

To make the woodpecker:
1 You will need a string fruit bag, a circle of cardboard and sections cut from an egg carton as shown. Glue on the egg carton eyes and the point for the beak. **2** Glue on the string bag for the woodpecker's topknot.

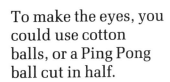

Your animal characters will look good mounted on a backing of cardboard.

Odds and ends at home may suggest other animals to try. A cow would need a black and white face, and cardboard horns. A donkey needs a long nose and ears, and a pink tongue.

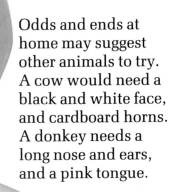

To make the eyes, you could use cotton balls, or a Ping Pong ball cut in half.

When your models are complete and the glue has dried, color the heads using bright poster paint (see page 54 for tips on paint). Place the models on a sheet of newspaper first, as painting can be messy.

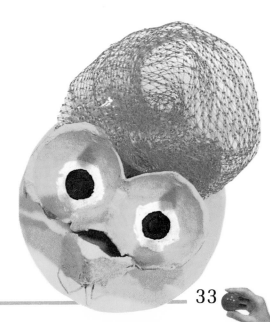

33

FARMYARD MOBILE

This mobile will look spectacular hung from a shelf or lampshade, where it can spin freely. Using your imagination, you can adapt these egg carton designs to make other zoo and farmyard animals.

STEP BY STEP

1 The bodies of the bee and pig are made from segments cut from an egg carton and taped together. **2** Cut the bee's wings from foil and tape them on. **3** To make the pig's snout, make a small hole in the end of the body. Insert the top of a dishwashing liquid bottle. **4** Pigs can sometimes fly. Cardboard wings have been taped to this one, and a wire tail is added. **5** Tape a long thread to the back of both animals. **6** The daffodils are made from tissue paper, straws and segments of candy box tray. **7** Cut the tissue paper into petal shapes.

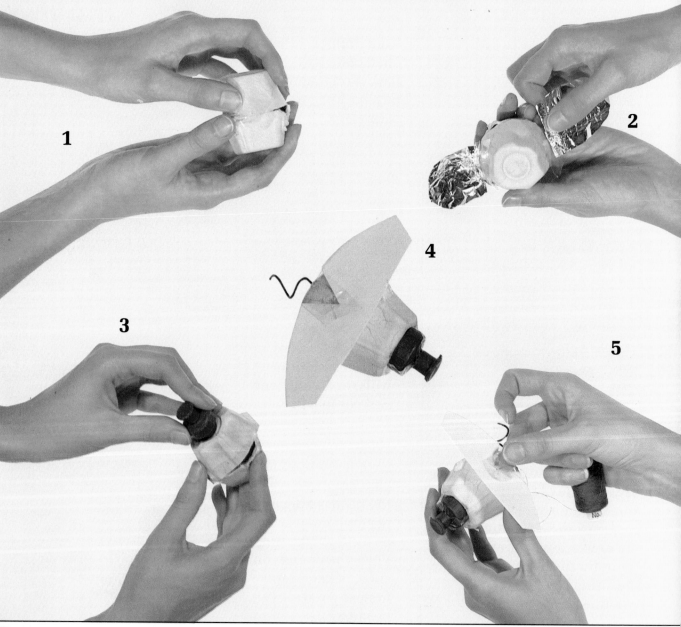

foil

drinking straws

thread

candy box tray

egg carton

Glue on straw stems and candy tray trumpets. **8** Bind two short pieces of garden stick with string, to form a cross. String the flowers and the animals from it. If the mobile isn't balanced, add modeling clay blobs to the models to even it up.

You can use a large paper clip to hook the model onto a shelf. You could also hang it on a string, so it can turn freely.

6

7

8

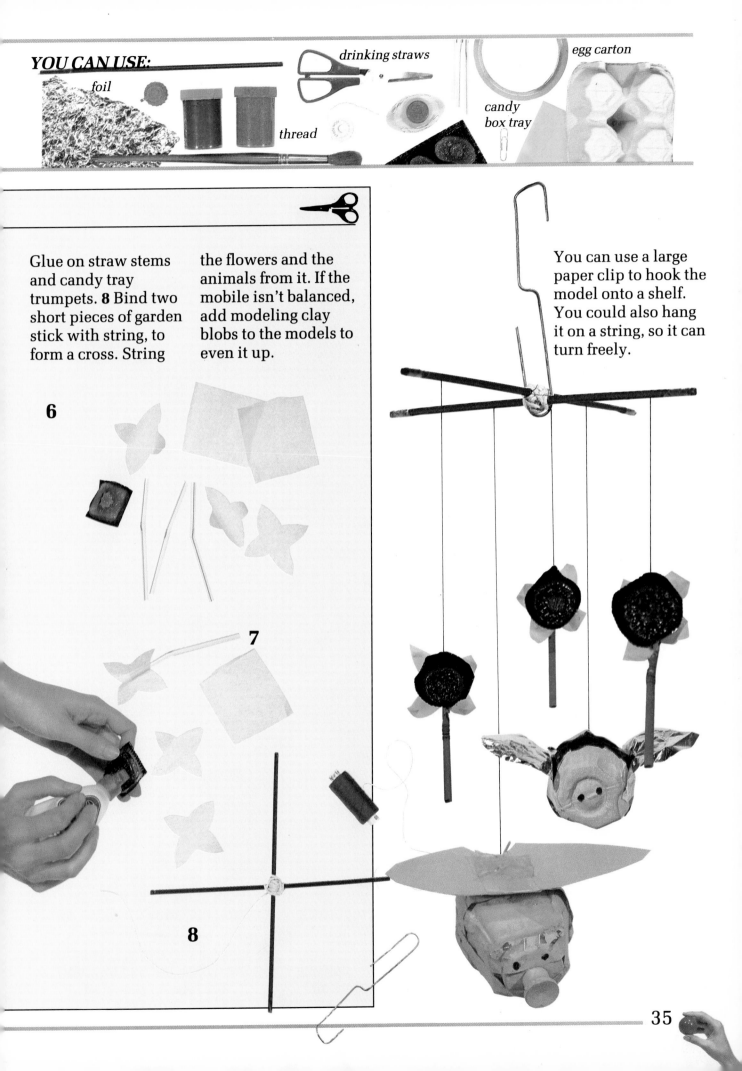

35

BOUNCING CANARY

The canary is easy to make and will bounce merrily from a window or bookshelf, flapping its wings. Its secret is an egg carton body weighted with modeling clay. You can adapt this design to make a spider or seagull.

STEP BY STEP

1 Cut two segments for the body and a point for the beak from an egg carton. Put modeling clay inside the body and tape it all together. **2** To make the eyes, pierce a hole in the side of two bottle tops. **3** Push a toothpick through one eye and then through the beak.
4 Push the other eye onto the end of the toothpick.

5 Cut short sections of bendable straws for the claws, and tape them to the body. **6** Cut paper shapes for the wings, tail and topknot. **7** Now tape on the wings,

YOU CAN USE: plastic bottle tops

rubber bands

toothpick

tissue paper

straws

egg carton

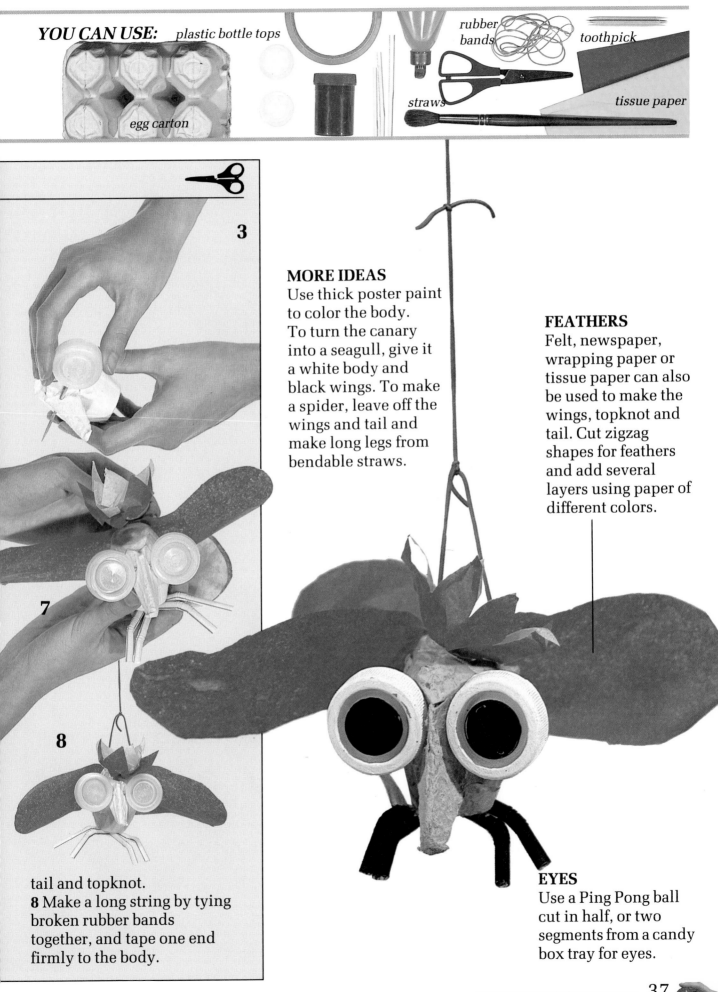

3

7

8

MORE IDEAS
Use thick poster paint
to color the body.
To turn the canary
into a seagull, give it
a white body and
black wings. To make
a spider, leave off the
wings and tail and
make long legs from
bendable straws.

FEATHERS
Felt, newspaper,
wrapping paper or
tissue paper can also
be used to make the
wings, topknot and
tail. Cut zigzag
shapes for feathers
and add several
layers using paper of
different colors.

EYES
Use a Ping Pong ball
cut in half, or two
segments from a candy
box tray for eyes.

tail and topknot.
8 Make a long string by tying
broken rubber bands
together, and tape one end
firmly to the body.

SLITHERY SNAKE

This colorful snake has a wriggly body made of yogurt cups. It will sway and twist in your hand in a lifelike manner. You could alter this design to make either a caterpillar or a crocodile.

STEP BY STEP

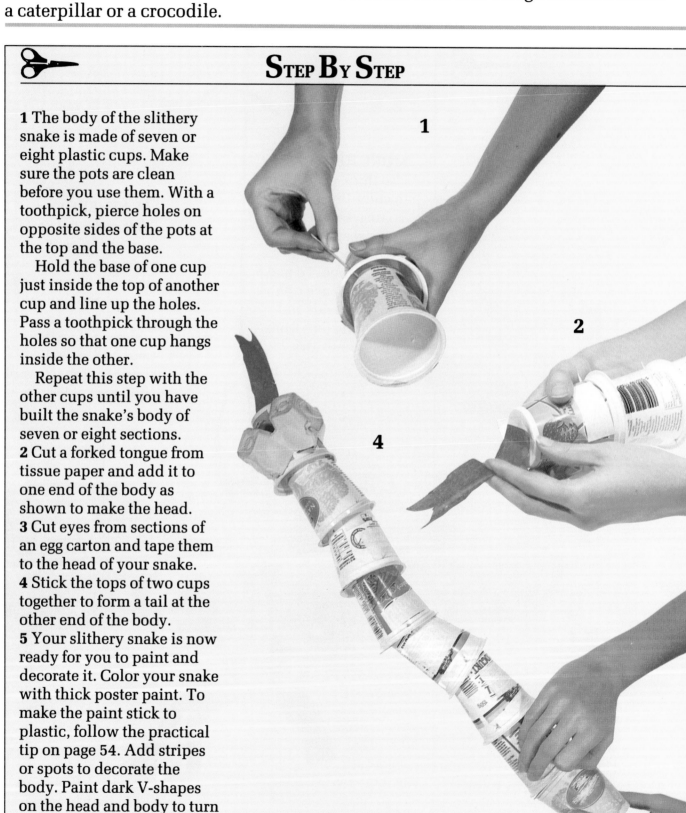

1 The body of the slithery snake is made of seven or eight plastic cups. Make sure the pots are clean before you use them. With a toothpick, pierce holes on opposite sides of the pots at the top and the base.

Hold the base of one cup just inside the top of another cup and line up the holes. Pass a toothpick through the holes so that one cup hangs inside the other.

Repeat this step with the other cups until you have built the snake's body of seven or eight sections.

2 Cut a forked tongue from tissue paper and add it to one end of the body as shown to make the head.

3 Cut eyes from sections of an egg carton and tape them to the head of your snake.

4 Stick the tops of two cups together to form a tail at the other end of the body.

5 Your slithery snake is now ready for you to paint and decorate it. Color your snake with thick poster paint. To make the paint stick to plastic, follow the practical tip on page 54. Add stripes or spots to decorate the body. Paint dark V-shapes on the head and body to turn your snake into a viper.

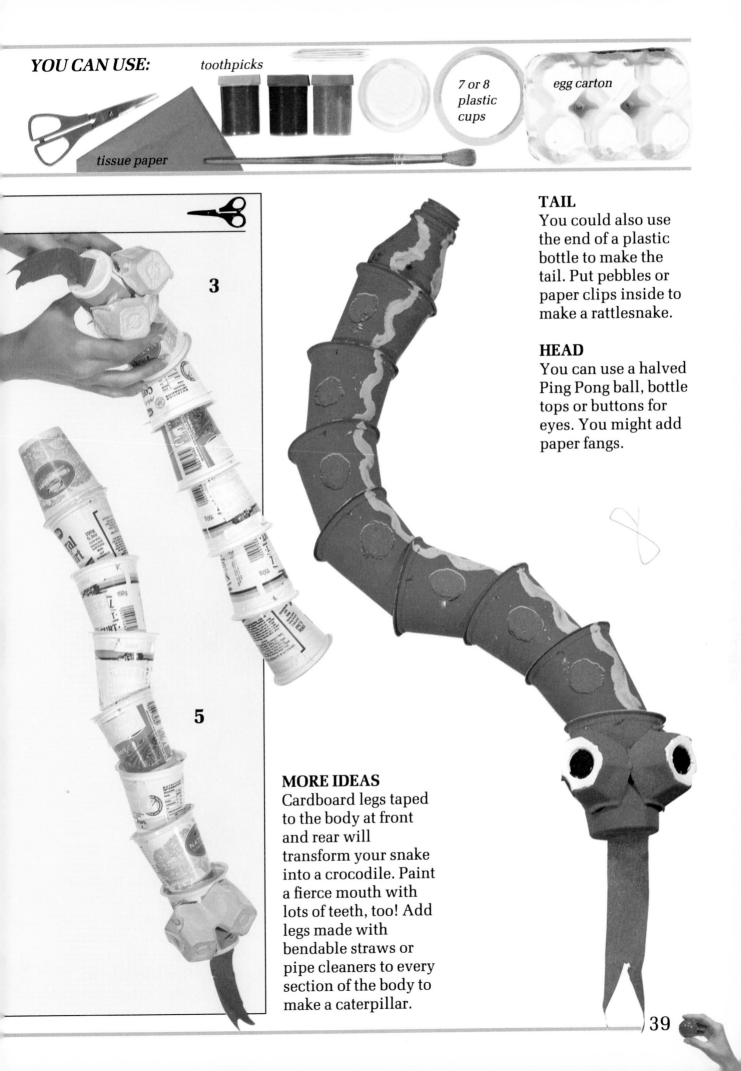

3

5

TAIL
You could also use the end of a plastic bottle to make the tail. Put pebbles or paper clips inside to make a rattlesnake.

HEAD
You can use a halved Ping Pong ball, bottle tops or buttons for eyes. You might add paper fangs.

MORE IDEAS
Cardboard legs taped to the body at front and rear will transform your snake into a crocodile. Paint a fierce mouth with lots of teeth, too! Add legs made with bendable straws or pipe cleaners to every section of the body to make a caterpillar.

NODDING BEAGLE

The nodding beagle has a head that rocks on a garden stick pivot. It will nod soulfully, from the back window of your family's car, perhaps. You can alter this design to make a rabbit instead.

This beagle's shaggy fringe is cut from the edge of a paper plate. You could glue on strands of yarn instead.

When the model is complete, color it with poster paint. Your beagle could be black or white with spots or patches, or you could choose a different breed.

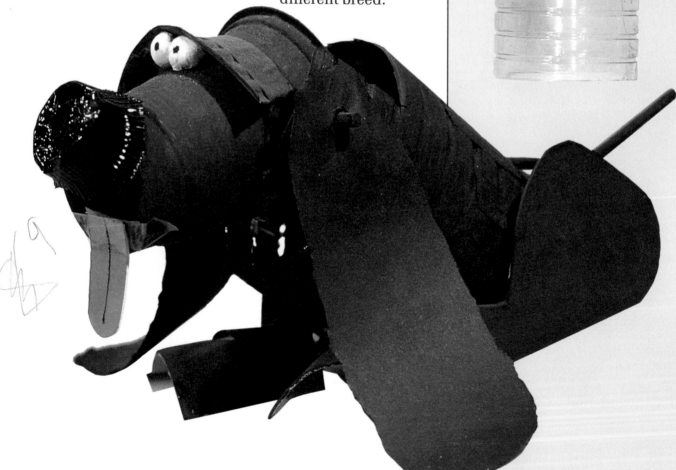

1

You could make a kennel for your beagle out of a clean milk carton or small box. Cut a doorway in one side to fit your model.

You can alter this design to make many different animals. For example, by adding long cardboard ears and a fluffy tail of cotton balls you can turn this model into a rabbit.

1 Cut out the middle section of a plastic bottle. Cut it again as shown, leaving two tabs to form the neck pivot. Pierce a hole through the center of each tab. **2** The beagle's head is a plastic cup

YOU CAN USE:

two toilet paper tubes

candy box tray

garden stick

straws

plastic cup

plastic bottle

STEP BY STEP

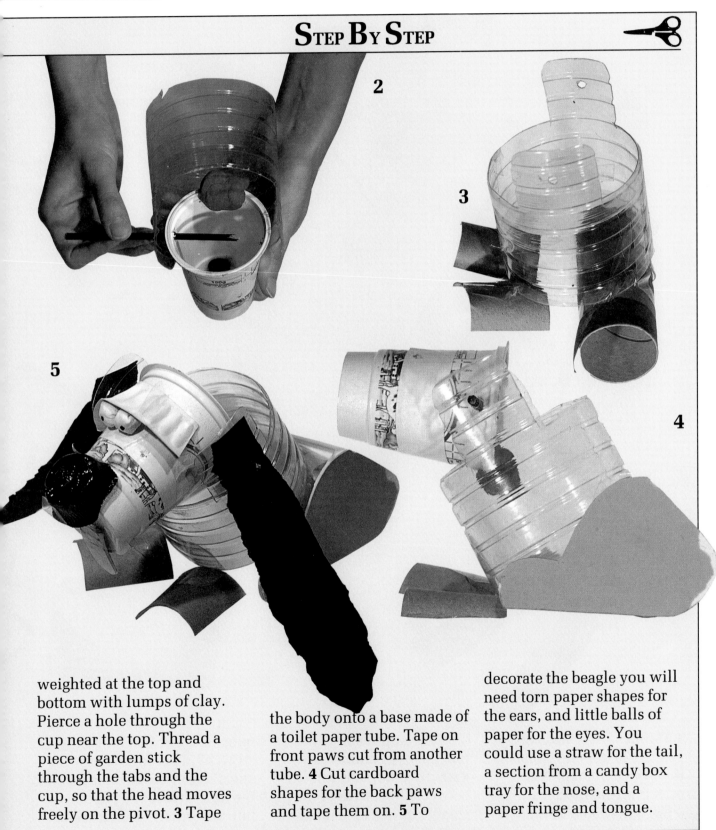

2

3

5

4

weighted at the top and bottom with lumps of clay. Pierce a hole through the cup near the top. Thread a piece of garden stick through the tabs and the cup, so that the head moves freely on the pivot. **3** Tape

the body onto a base made of a toilet paper tube. Tape on front paws cut from another tube. **4** Cut cardboard shapes for the back paws and tape them on. **5** To

decorate the beagle you will need torn paper shapes for the ears, and little balls of paper for the eyes. You could use a straw for the tail, a section from a candy box tray for the nose, and a paper fringe and tongue.

41

MONKEY PUPPET

This monkey is a marionette, or string puppet. It is easy to make and great fun to operate. This design can be altered to make an elephant, and many other animals – the choice is yours!

STEP BY STEP

1 Tape a small cardboard box to a larger one to make the head and body. **2** Cut eyes from an egg carton. **3** Cut a large and a small circle of cardboard. Cut the circles in half. **4** Tape a strip of colored tissue between the halves of the smaller circle, to make the muzzle. **5** Cut two long thin strips of paper for the arms, and shorter, wider ones for the legs. Crease the paper into accordion folds and add

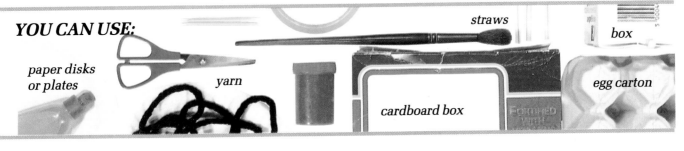

paper disks or plates

yarn

cardboard box

straws

box

egg carton

4

7

Paint your puppet with poster paint. You could add a tail of paper with accordion folds, and a hat made from a plastic cup.

straws for fingers and toes.
6 Tape onto the head the eyes, muzzle, and the halves of the larger circle to form the ears. Tape the arms and legs onto the body. Glue on a paper plate for the tummy.
7 Decorate your monkey with yarn hair.

This design can be altered to make many other animals. You could make an elephant, with a long trunk made of plastic cups linked with toothpicks (see pages 38-39). Paint the elephant gray with pink toenails.

43

STRINGING THE MONKEY PUPPET

Complete your monkey marionette by stringing it to a frame. You could team up with a friend and make other animal puppets. Invent an adventure for the puppets, and then put on a performance for your family and friends.

STEP BY STEP

1 To string your puppet you will need two short pieces of garden stake, and four lengths of string: a long piece for the body, two medium lengths for the arms, and a short piece for the head. Make the frame by binding the sticks into a cross with string. Tie the strings to the frame. Attach the arm strings to opposite points of the cross, and tie the short head string to the middle. **2** Tape the arm strings firmly to the puppet's wrists. **3** Tape the body string to the base of the back. **4** Tape on the head string.

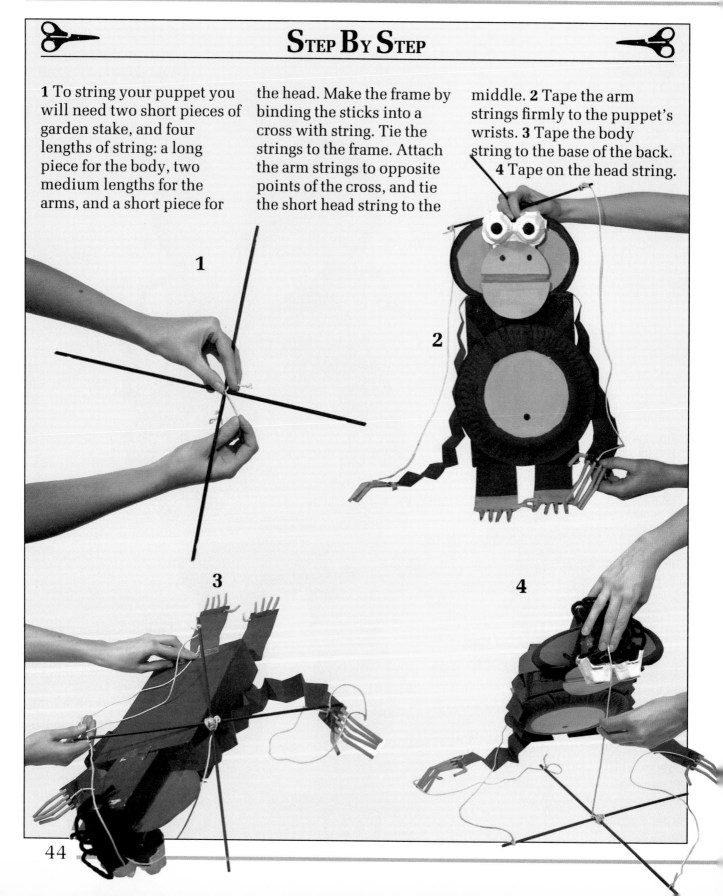

cotton thread
or string

sticks or garden stakes

tape

scissors

Tilt the frame to one side, or lift the arm strings one at a time to make the puppet wave or beckon. Tilt the frame from side to side to give it a swaggering walking movement. Dip the front of the frame in order to make your puppet bow.

Practice moving the crossframe to make your puppet jump and dance.

45

TORTOISE BANK

The shell of this tortoise is made from papier mâché, a term which comes from the French words for mashed paper. Papier mâché can be messy, so wear old clothes and cover your work surface with newspaper.

STEP BY STEP

1 In a bowl, mix flour and water to make a thick paste. **2** Blow up a balloon and stand it in a bowl. Tear a newspaper into strips, and dip a strip in the paste. Run

the strip through your fingers to remove excess paste. Lay the strip over the balloon. Continue until the top half of the balloon is covered with at least three layers of newspaper.

3 Leave the papier mâché shell until it is dry. Burst the balloon. Trim the bottom flat with scissors, and make a slit in the top. **4** Cut short slits in the neck

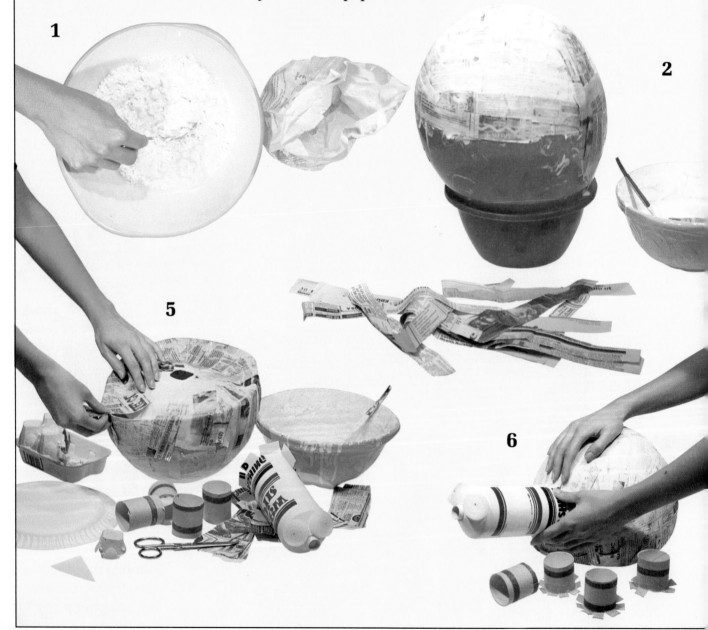

46

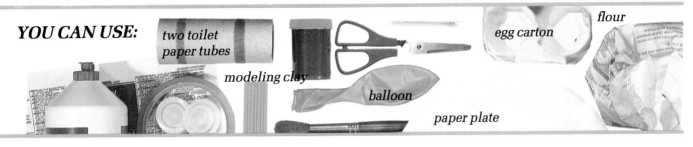

YOU CAN USE: two toilet paper tubes

modeling clay

scissors

balloon

paper plate

egg carton

flour

of the plastic bottle, to make flaps (see page 54). Pin on two plastic bottle tops for eyes. **5** The base of the tortoise is a paper plate. Cut a section from an egg carton to make the plug. Cut a hole in the paper plate to fit it. Papier mâché the plate onto the shell.

To finish the tortoise:
6 Attach the head to the body with tape or papier mâché. **7** Cut flaps in the feet and attach them to the body in the same way.

Give your tortoise a mottled shell as shown here. Add clay pupils to the eyes, and a cardboard tail.

Your savings can be kept in the tortoise bank. When you want to spend them, simply remove the plug.

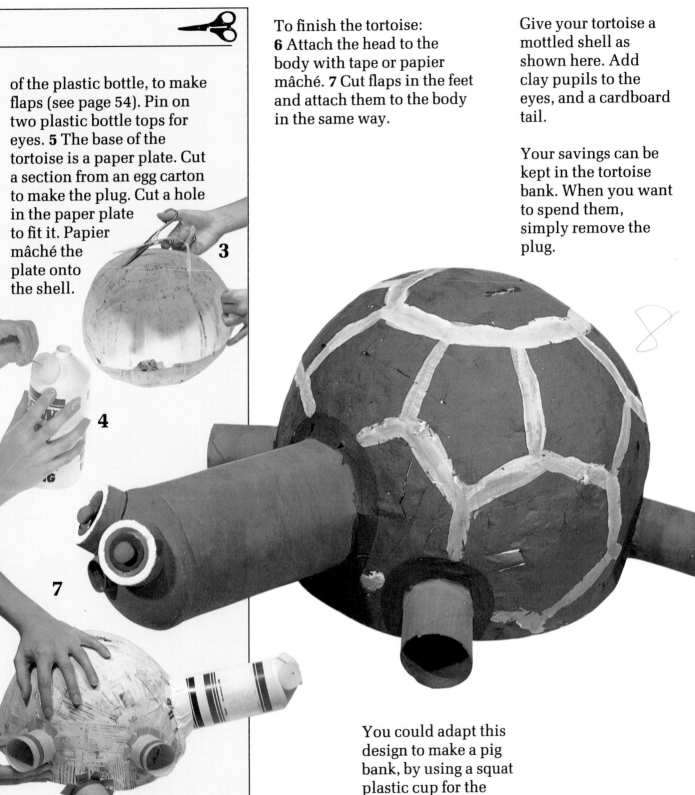

You could adapt this design to make a pig bank, by using a squat plastic cup for the nose. Add floppy cardboard ears, too.

SHAPELY SWAN

This graceful bird is a simple project which uses only newspaper and cardboard to construct a sturdy frame. You can use the same design to make a Canada goose or a farmyard duck.

1 To make the swan's body, you will need to scrunch several sheets of newspaper into a large, tight ball, and tape it together. Tape up another sheet into a long, tight roll. You will also need two small paper disks, a larger paper circle with a quarter section cut out, and a thin cardboard strip cut as shown. Cut cardboard wings using the help of the pattern on pages 56-57.
2 Flatten and tape one end of the newspaper roll under the body and at the base of the neck. **3** Wind the other end of the roll around a pencil to create a tight curl. Tape it tightly together.
4 Take the large paper disk with the quarter section removed and tape the sides together to make a cone. Then tape the cone to the body to make the tail.
5 Hold the wings under the body. Crease them up around the body and tape them on. **6** Draw eyes on the two paper circles and glue or tape them to the head. To make the beak, fold the thin strip of cardboard you cut earlier. The fold is trimmed to form the point of the beak. Run the ends of the strip around either side of the head and tape them in place.

YOU CAN USE:

newspaper

scissors

pen

tape

cardboard

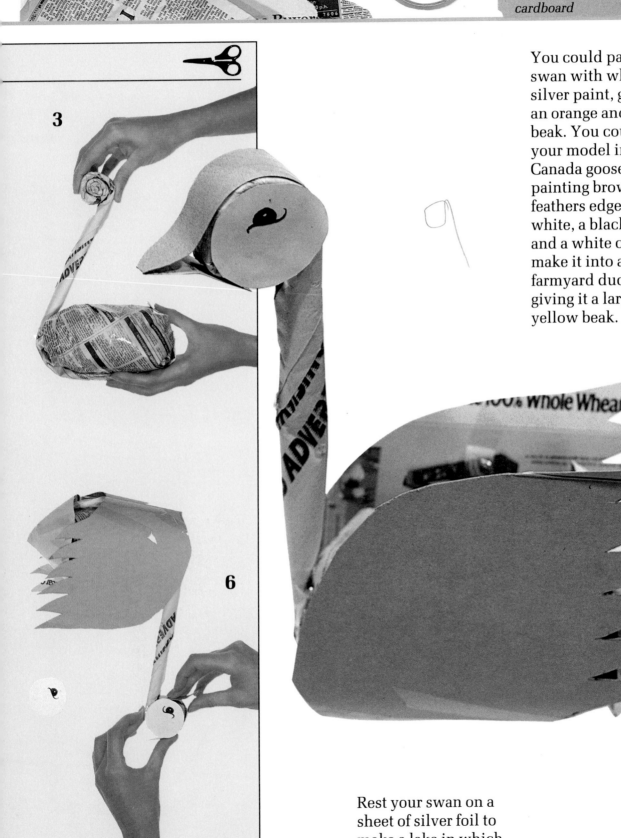

3

6

You could paint your
swan with white or
silver paint, giving it
an orange and black
beak. You could make
your model into a
Canada goose by
painting brown
feathers edged with
white, a black head
and a white chest. Or
make it into a
farmyard duck by
giving it a large round
yellow beak.

Rest your swan on a
sheet of silver foil to
make a lake in which
it will be reflected.

49

CRANKY CAMEL

This lordly animal is made by laying papier mâché over a newspaper frame, using the techniques you used to make the swan and tortoise. The camel is decorated with a paper saddle, and you can also add reins.

1 Tightly roll up three sheets of newspaper. Tape them so they don't unfurl. Scrunch up three newspaper balls, and a smaller ball. Tape them up in the same way. Make a frame for the body by folding two long rolls over the third. You could secure them in position with tape. If the ends of the legs are uneven, even them up with scissors.

2 Bend the neck up and tape the end tightly around the small newspaper ball to make the camel's head.

3 Tape the three balls to the back to make the hump.

4 Tear a newspaper into strips. Prepare a flour and water paste for papier mâché, as you did to make the tortoise bank (see pages 46-47). Cover the whole frame with at least three layers of newspaper strips. Support the model by looping and tying string around the legs. Leave it to dry overnight. Your camel is now ready for you to paint and decorate it.

5 To make the saddle, decorate a rectangle of paper with paints or crayons. Cut four slits in it to fit over your camel's hump. Fold and tape it around the hump.

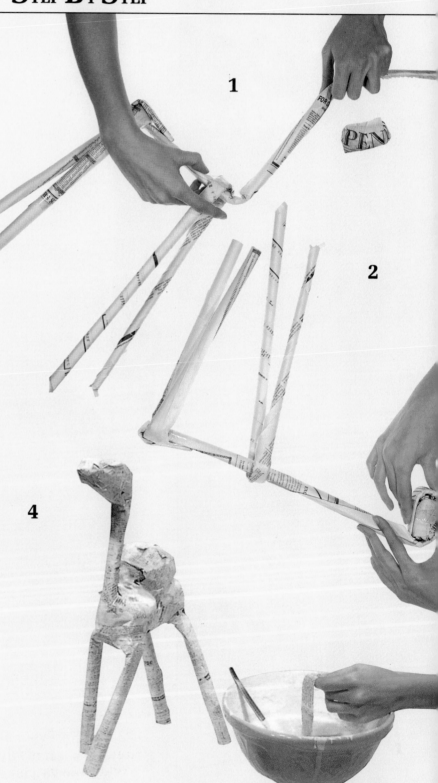

YOU CAN USE:

tape

string

flour
and
water

newspaper

3

5

Color the camel's body with bright poster paint. You could add paper ears, and paint on long eyelashes and a cranky expression. You could add reins and a tail of string, yarn, or cord.

You could decorate the saddle with sequins or glitter. You could also string saddlebags made with plastic cups across the saddle.

PROUD PEACOCK AND GIRAFFE

The techniques described on the previous page can be used to make all kinds of animals. By changing the size of the body or the number of limbs, you can make a peacock, a giraffe, or any animal you choose.

STEP BY STEP

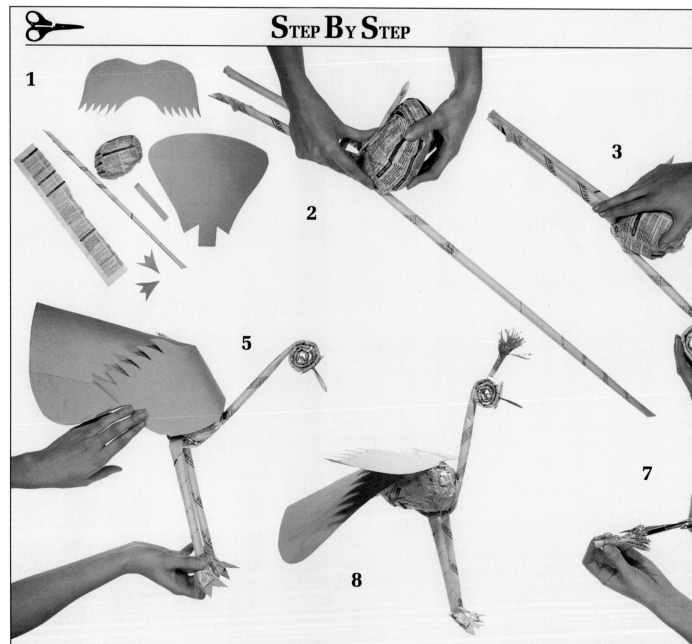

1 To make the peacock, make a large newspaper ball and two long rolls. Cut cardboard shapes for the wings, feet and tail, using the patterns on pages 56-57.
2 The peacock is similar to the swan on pages 48-49. Tape the longest roll around the body. Loop in the other roll for the legs.
3 Curl the neck around a pencil to make the head. Fold and tape on a small cardboard strip for the beak.
4 Fold and tape the tail around the body.
5 Tape on the wings. Fold the legs over and then tape on the feet.
6 To make the topknot, roll up a long, thin strip of newspaper.
7 Cut a series of slits around one end. Unroll and reroll it, tape it together and tape it to the peacock's head.

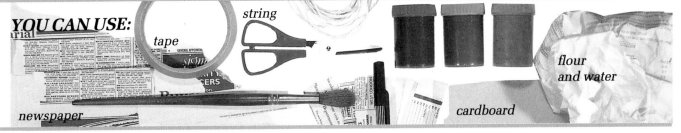

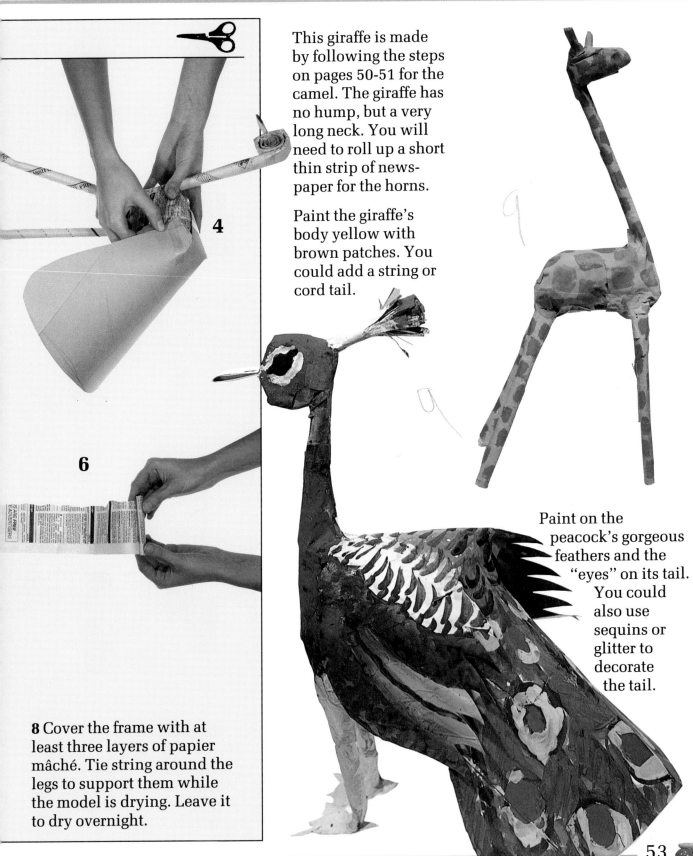

4

6

This giraffe is made by following the steps on pages 50-51 for the camel. The giraffe has no hump, but a very long neck. You will need to roll up a short thin strip of newspaper for the horns.

Paint the giraffe's body yellow with brown patches. You could add a string or cord tail.

Paint on the peacock's gorgeous feathers and the "eyes" on its tail. You could also use sequins or glitter to decorate the tail.

8 Cover the frame with at least three layers of papier mâché. Tie string around the legs to support them while the model is drying. Leave it to dry overnight.

53

PRACTICAL TIPS

Below are a few practical hints that will help you with some of the projects described in this book.

CREATING FLAPS

Use this tip for attaching the head and legs of your tortoise bank (see pages 46-47) and for fastening tube shapes onto your models.

Attaching a tube is easy if you use scissors to cut a number of short slits around one end of the tube first.

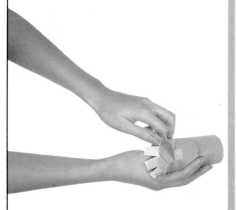

The slits form a series of flaps. Bend the flaps outward. Now you can press the tube flat onto the surface of your model. Use glue, tape, or papier mâché to attach the tube to the model.

CUTTING A HOLE

This hint will help you make the pig for your farmyard mobile (see pages 34-35) and the base of your tortoise bank (pages 46-47). It is a useful technique whenever you need to make a hole in the middle of a piece of paper or cardboard, without cutting in from the edge. Place the paper shape that you want to cut out over a soft surface, such as an eraser.

Use a sharp pencil to pierce through the middle of your shape. You will now be able to insert the point of your scissors into the hole. Cut to the edge of the paper shape, and then cut around the shape with scissors.

PAINTING

It may be difficult to get poster paint to stick to plastic. This tip will help.

Poster paint will stick to plastic if you squirt a little dishwashing liquid into your mixing water. Stir it around with your brush before you begin.

PAPER: comics and magazines, postcards and birthday cards, unused wallpaper, tissue.

MORE JUNK IDEAS

The materials used most often in this book have been paper, cardboard and plastic packaging. Below are some more suggestions about the kinds of junk which can be used to make and decorate your models.

WOOD: spent matches, garden stakes, cotton spools, lollypop sticks.

FABRIC: yarn, socks, old clothes or sheets, cloth and felt scraps.

PLASTIC: food containers, candy and snack wrappers, buttons, broken toys.

RUBBER: rubber bands, balls, balloons, old rubber gloves.

METAL: soft drink cans, foil, springs, pipe cleaners, hangers, paper clips.

PATTERNS

Below are patterns that will help with some of the projects in this book. You will need a pencil and thin paper or tracing paper.

To use these patterns, follow the steps shown at the top of the opposite page.

1 Trace the pattern shape onto tracing paper.

2 Turn the tracing over, and place it on top of the paper or cardboard on which you want the image to appear. Scribble over the lines showing through the paper with your pencil. A mirror image of the pattern will appear on the cardboard.

3 If you want the image to appear the right way around, turn the tracing paper over again, and place it over paper or cardboard.

4 Draw carefully over your tracing again.

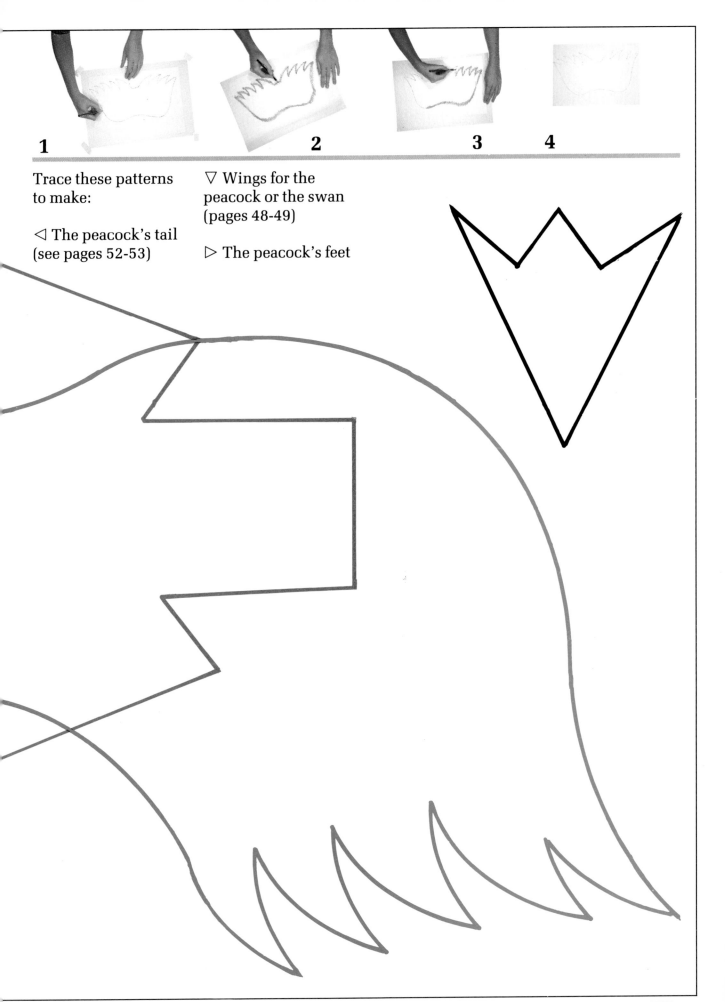

Trace these patterns
to make:

◁ The peacock's tail
(see pages 52-53)

▽ Wings for the
peacock or the swan
(pages 48-49)

▷ The peacock's feet

POWERED SPEEDBOAT

This simply-made speedboat with its racing crew will make waves in a pond or swimming pool, or even in the bath! Powered by a balloon, the boat will streak across the water as if jet-propelled.

1 Using a pair of scissors, cut a clean plastic bottle in half lengthwise.
2 Pierce the back of the boat with scissors. Enlarge the hole to fit the neck of a balloon. To make the boat watertight at the front, cut a triangular-shaped wedge of plastic from the part of the bottle you have discarded. Crease it down the middle and attach it to the neck of the bottle with tape, to act as a prow.
3 Push the neck of the balloon through the hole you have made in the rear of the boat. You will need to weight the boat to prevent it from capsizing. Line the front of the boat with a lump of modeling clay, and make clay passengers. Place them in the prow (front) of the boat too, to provide more stability.

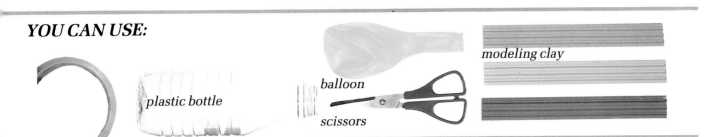

YOU CAN USE:

plastic bottle

balloon

scissors

modeling clay

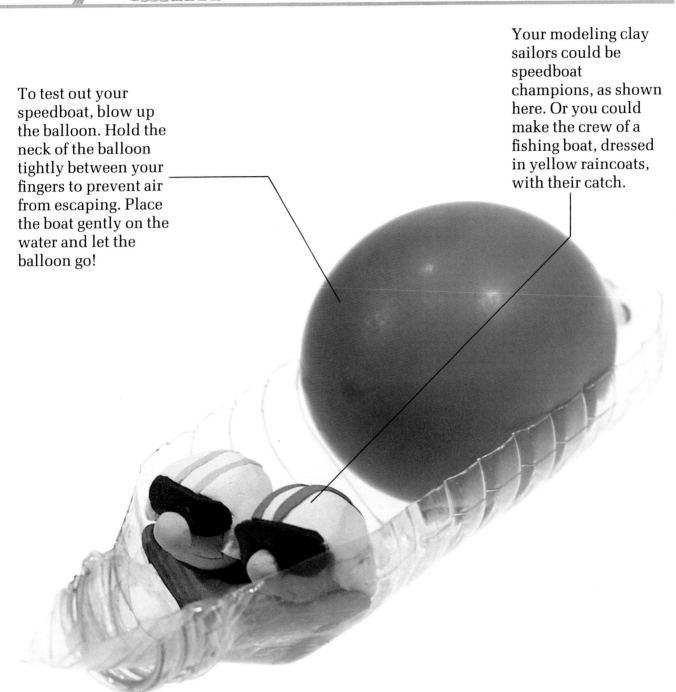

To test out your speedboat, blow up the balloon. Hold the neck of the balloon tightly between your fingers to prevent air from escaping. Place the boat gently on the water and let the balloon go!

Your modeling clay sailors could be speedboat champions, as shown here. Or you could make the crew of a fishing boat, dressed in yellow raincoats, with their catch.

You could add a ship's wheel at the front. Your boat can also carry small plastic toys.

VIKING LONGBOAT

Viking warriors sailed the seas in the 9th and 10th centuries, on raiding missions around the coasts of Europe. Their ships had carved figureheads of monsters or serpents. This longboat design can be adapted to make a pirate ship.

STEP BY STEP

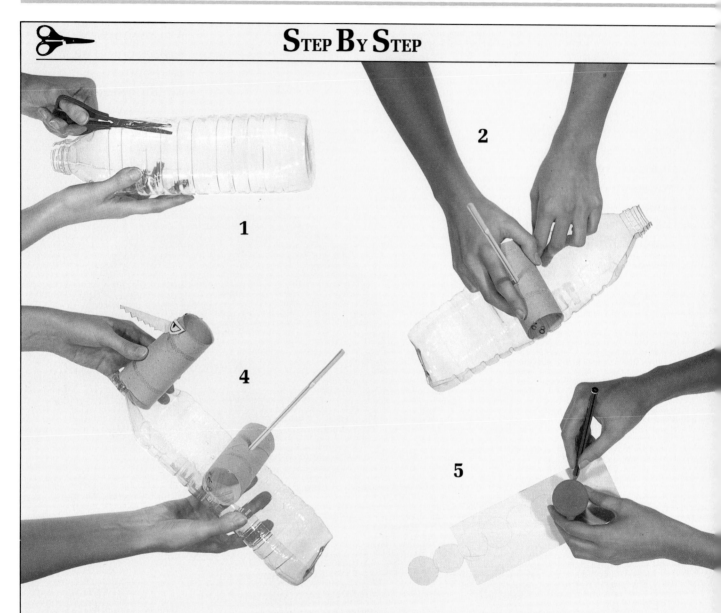

1 To make the longboat, cut a plastic bottle in half lengthwise with scissors.
2 Make a hole in a toilet paper tube. Push a straw into the hole for the mast. Wedge the tube sideways into the boat. Trim the tube if it doesn't fit.
3 Viking ships had fierce figureheads. Yours will be made with a second cardboard tube. Cut a pointed beak for it from cardboard or from the inside of an egg carton. Cut fierce-looking teeth into the beak, and glue or tape it to the tube.
4 Draw scowling eyes with a felt-tip pen. Cut them out and glue or tape them on too. Wedge the figurehead in the front of the boat.
5 Draw around a small bottle to create two rows of linked circles. Cut them out and stick them to the sides of your longboat to form two lines of Viking shields.
6 Make a sail with a square of paper or thin cardboard. Cut small slits near the top

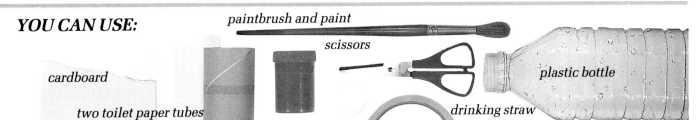

YOU CAN USE:

paintbrush and paint

scissors

cardboard

two toilet paper tubes

drinking straw

plastic bottle

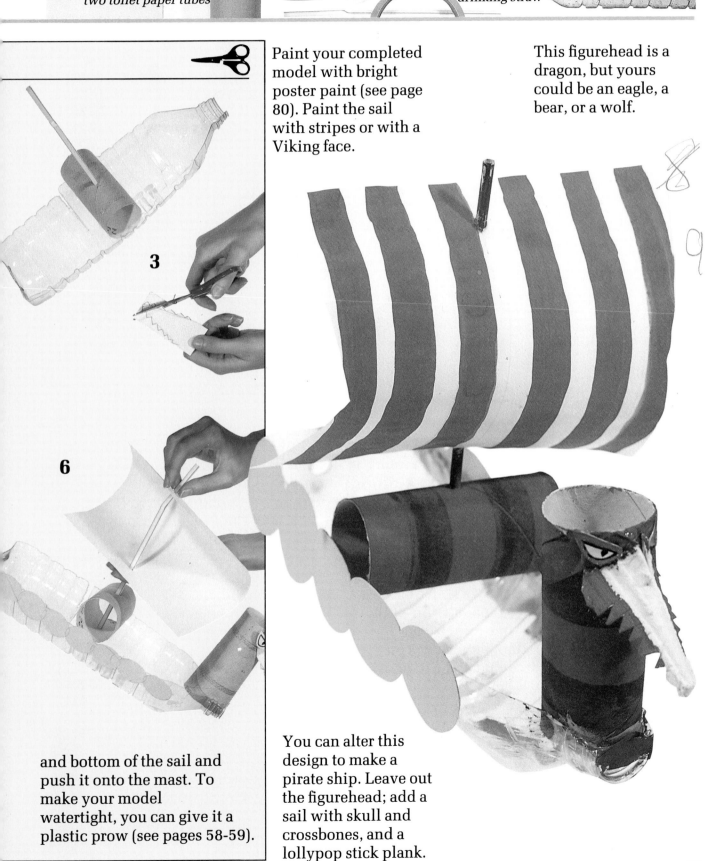

3

6

Paint your completed model with bright poster paint (see page 80). Paint the sail with stripes or with a Viking face.

This figurehead is a dragon, but yours could be an eagle, a bear, or a wolf.

and bottom of the sail and push it onto the mast. To make your model watertight, you can give it a plastic prow (see pages 58-59).

You can alter this design to make a pirate ship. Leave out the figurehead; add a sail with skull and crossbones, and a lollypop stick plank.

SPACE ROCKET

This spaceship has three stages that fit together and will be detached during a space flight. The third stage, jettisoned after launch, and the command module have rocket boosters for powering the craft on space missions.

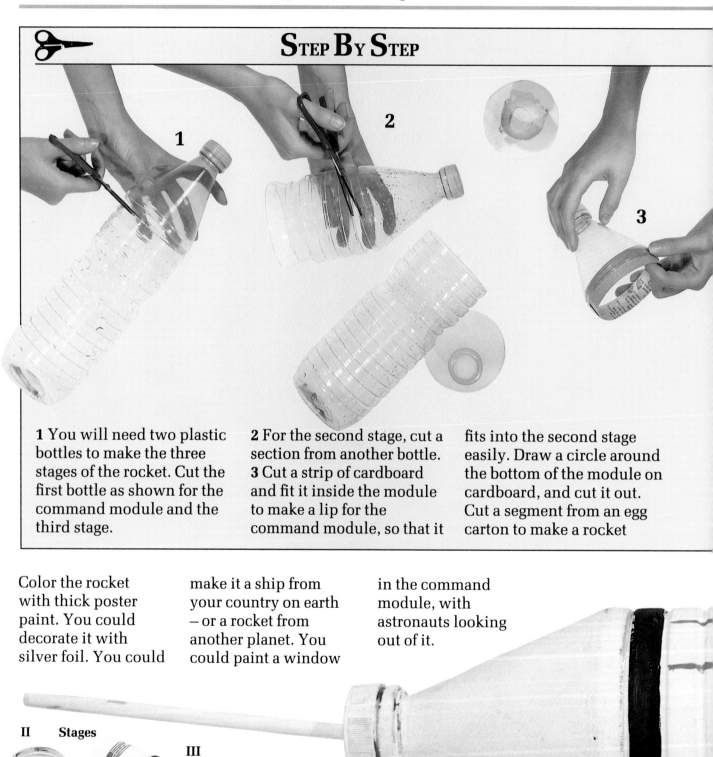

STEP BY STEP

1 You will need two plastic bottles to make the three stages of the rocket. Cut the first bottle as shown for the command module and the third stage.

2 For the second stage, cut a section from another bottle.
3 Cut a strip of cardboard and fit it inside the module to make a lip for the command module, so that it

fits into the second stage easily. Draw a circle around the bottom of the module on cardboard, and cut it out. Cut a segment from an egg carton to make a rocket

Color the rocket with thick poster paint. You could decorate it with silver foil. You could

make it a ship from your country on earth – or a rocket from another planet. You could paint a window

in the command module, with astronauts looking out of it.

II   **Stages**

III

I

62

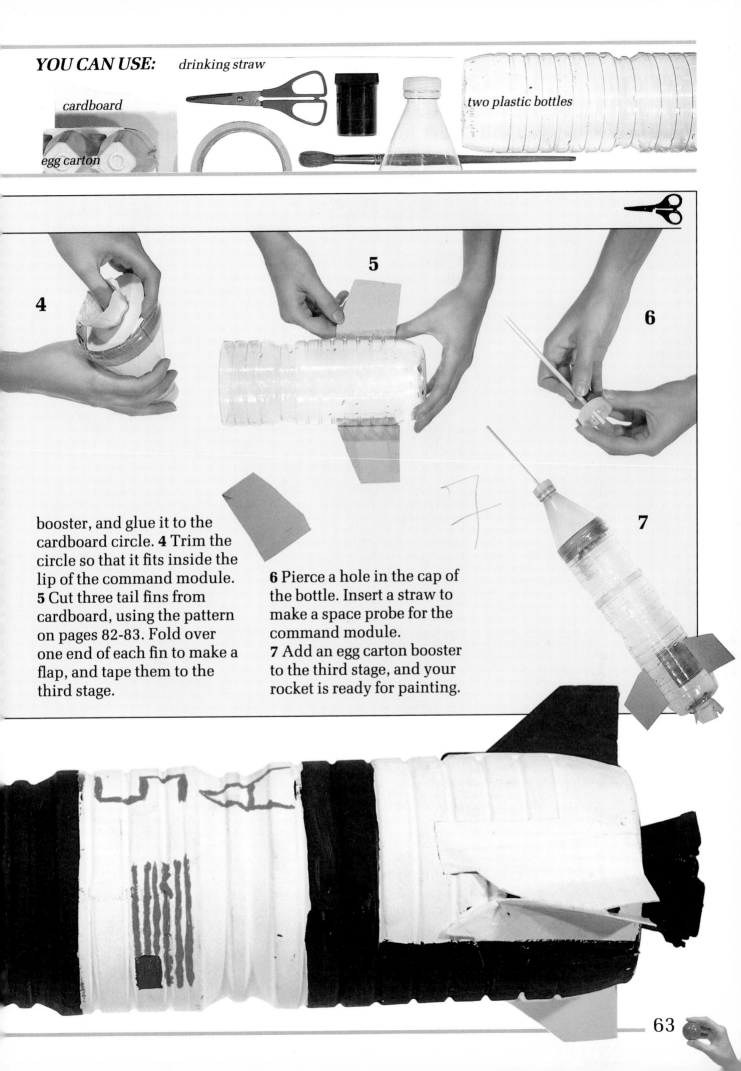

4

5

6

7

booster, and glue it to the cardboard circle. **4** Trim the circle so that it fits inside the lip of the command module. **5** Cut three tail fins from cardboard, using the pattern on pages 82-83. Fold over one end of each fin to make a flap, and tape them to the third stage.

6 Pierce a hole in the cap of the bottle. Insert a straw to make a space probe for the command module.
7 Add an egg carton booster to the third stage, and your rocket is ready for painting.

TWO-WAY TELEPHONE

These colorful telephones are easy to make and great fun to operate. When the line is pulled taut you will be able to hear a friend's voice and speak to him or her in the next room – or as far away as your string will stretch!

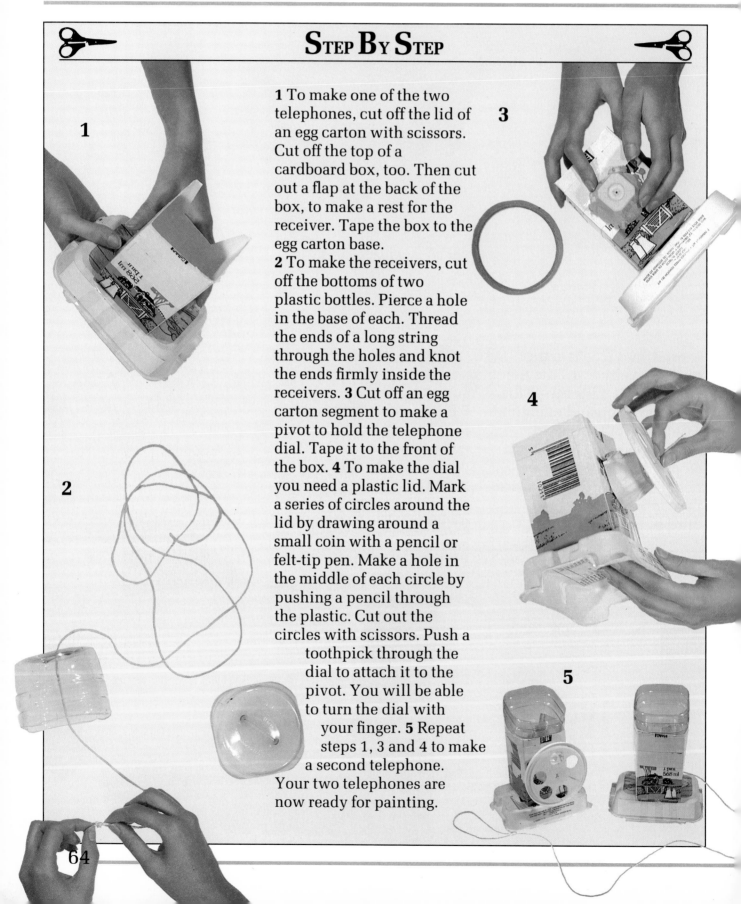

1 To make one of the two telephones, cut off the lid of an egg carton with scissors. Cut off the top of a cardboard box, too. Then cut out a flap at the back of the box, to make a rest for the receiver. Tape the box to the egg carton base.

2 To make the receivers, cut off the bottoms of two plastic bottles. Pierce a hole in the base of each. Thread the ends of a long string through the holes and knot the ends firmly inside the receivers. **3** Cut off an egg carton segment to make a pivot to hold the telephone dial. Tape it to the front of the box. **4** To make the dial you need a plastic lid. Mark a series of circles around the lid by drawing around a small coin with a pencil or felt-tip pen. Make a hole in the middle of each circle by pushing a pencil through the plastic. Cut out the circles with scissors. Push a toothpick through the dial to attach it to the pivot. You will be able to turn the dial with your finger. **5** Repeat steps 1, 3 and 4 to make a second telephone. Your two telephones are now ready for painting.

YOU CAN USE:

two plastic
bottles

two
plastic
lids

string

two cardboard
boxes

two
egg cartons

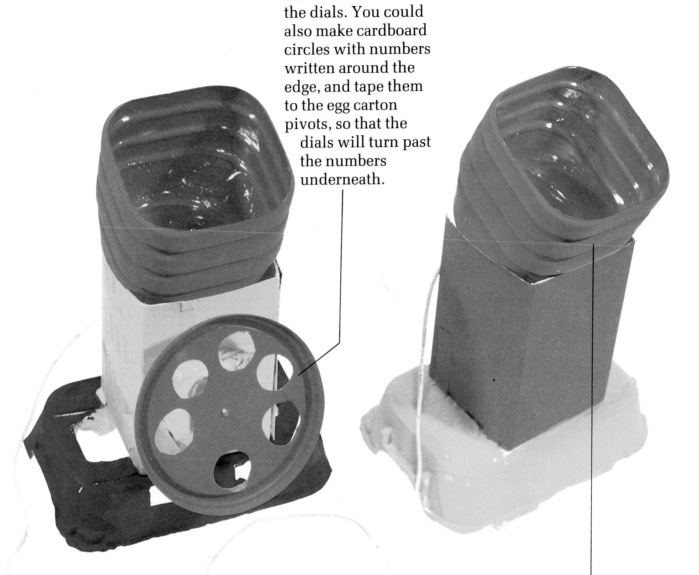

You could use cardboard to make the dials. You could also make cardboard circles with numbers written around the edge, and tape them to the egg carton pivots, so that the dials will turn past the numbers underneath.

You could also make the receivers from plastic cups.

To operate the telephones, stretch the cord tight and speak into the receiver while your friend has their ear to the other receiver.

Paint the telephone sets with bright poster paint. You could paint the working parts in different colors, as shown here.

INSTANT CAMERA

This trick camera contains an "instant photo" which you can use to surprise your friends. Pretend to take their picture, wait a moment to give the picture time to "develop," then produce the photo from your camera with a flourish!

STEP BY STEP

tops. Use toothpicks to pin them to the top and side of the camera body. Glue or tape a large plastic cup to the front for the lens.

3 Make a viewfinder by cutting a section from a cardboard tube as shown. Fold the sides to make two flaps. Make a small square hole in the middle.

1 In order to make the camera body, cut off the lids of two egg cartons and tape them together.

2 To make dials, pierce the middles of two plastic bottle

4 Glue the flaps to the camera body.

5 Make the backing for your "instant photo" by cutting a cardboard square, leaving one longer edge.

6 Find a photo you like in a magazine. Place the backing cardboard over it and trace around it with a pencil. Cut

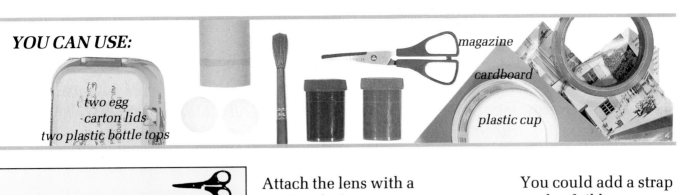

two egg
carton lids
two plastic bottle tops

magazine

cardboard

plastic cup

Attach the lens with a toothpick if you would like it to turn, as the other dials do.

You could add a strap made of ribbon, yarn, or string. Tape the strap to the camera so that you can wear the camera around your neck.

4

7

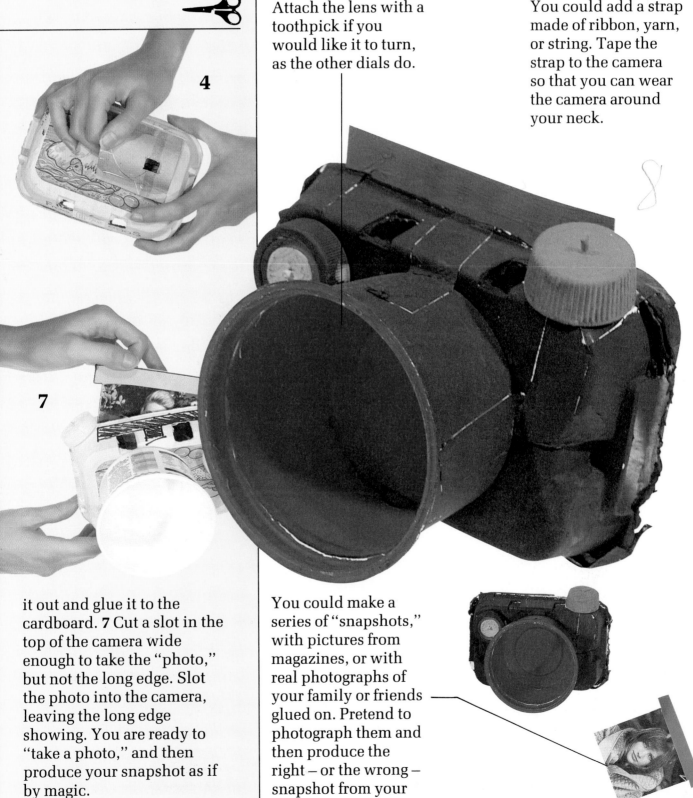

it out and glue it to the cardboard. **7** Cut a slot in the top of the camera wide enough to take the "photo," but not the long edge. Slot the photo into the camera, leaving the long edge showing. You are ready to "take a photo," and then produce your snapshot as if by magic.

You could make a series of "snapshots," with pictures from magazines, or with real photographs of your family or friends glued on. Pretend to photograph them and then produce the right – or the wrong – snapshot from your camera.

67

FLYING SAUCER WITH LAUNCHPAD

Do you believe that flying saucers have ever visited Earth? Many people do. This model, made with paper plates, works like a frisbee, and a flick of your wrist will send it skimming into space.

1

2

3

4

5

1 Make the saucer by taping together two paper plates. Cut off the bottom of a plastic bottle. **2** Make a series of circles by drawing around a circular object on cardboard. Cut out and cover the circles with silver foil. **3** Tape the bottom of the plastic bottle to your saucer, to make a viewing deck. (You could paint the plate inside the viewing deck before you tape it down securely). Tape the foil circles around the viewing deck. **4** To make the launch pad, cut off the bottom of another plastic bottle. Pierce three holes evenly spaced around the rim. Push straws through the holes to make the legs. Tape the straws inside the rim. **5** Push a toothpick into the top of the viewing deck of the flying machine to make an aerial.

YOU CAN USE:

cardboard

two plastic bottles

toothpick

straws *silver foil*

two paper plates

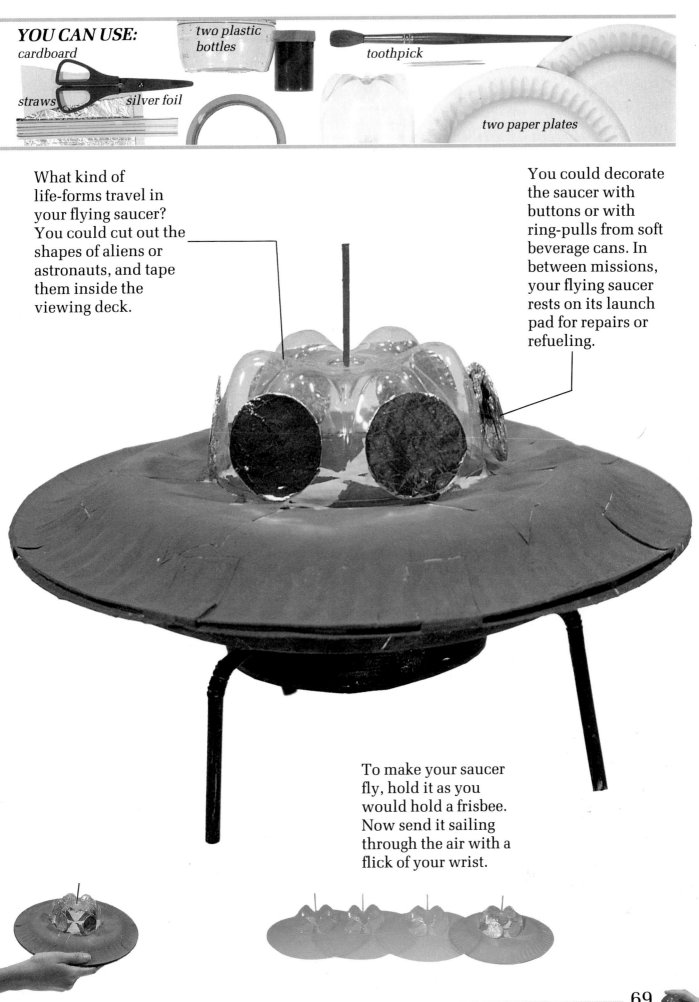

What kind of life-forms travel in your flying saucer? You could cut out the shapes of aliens or astronauts, and tape them inside the viewing deck.

You could decorate the saucer with buttons or with ring-pulls from soft beverage cans. In between missions, your flying saucer rests on its launch pad for repairs or refueling.

To make your saucer fly, hold it as you would hold a frisbee. Now send it sailing through the air with a flick of your wrist.

TELEVISION

This television is fitted with a scroll that you can turn to make images move across the screen. Cut out the pictures you want to appear on screen and put on a show to impress your family and friends.

STEP BY STEP

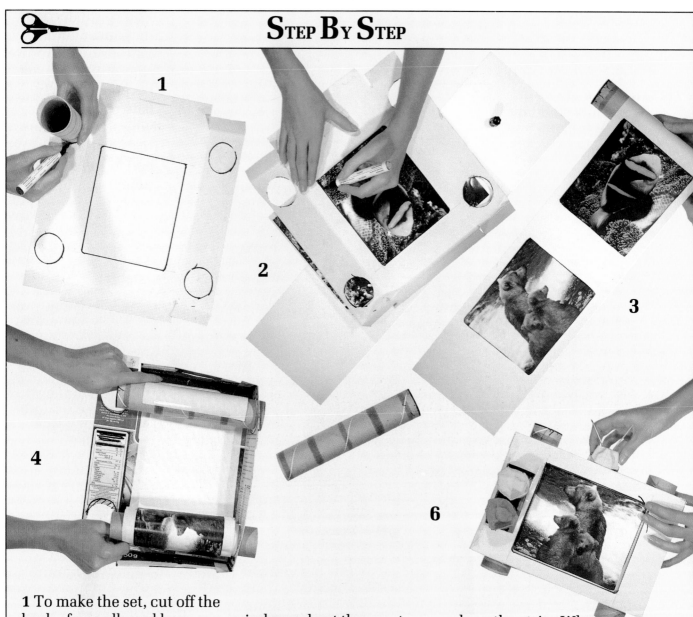

1 To make the set, cut off the back of a cardboard box, leaving the front, top, bottom, and sides. Mark a distance of 1 in from both ends of each side. You will need two paper towel tubes to make the scroll. Put the edge of one of the tubes where you've marked. Trace around it with a felt-tip pen. Pierce the center of the circles and cut them out.

2 Choose pictures you want to appear on screen from comics or magazines. Cut them out. Mark a screen to fit your pictures on the front of the box, and cut it out.

3 To make the scroll, you need a long strip of paper that just fits inside your television. Glue the pictures along the strip. When the glue is dry, roll the strip around the cardboard tubes. Secure the ends to the rolls with tape.

4 Fit the scroll inside the television, pushing the ends of the tubes through the holes in the box.

5 Secure the ends outside the box with toothpicks.

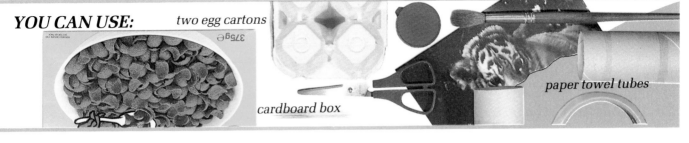

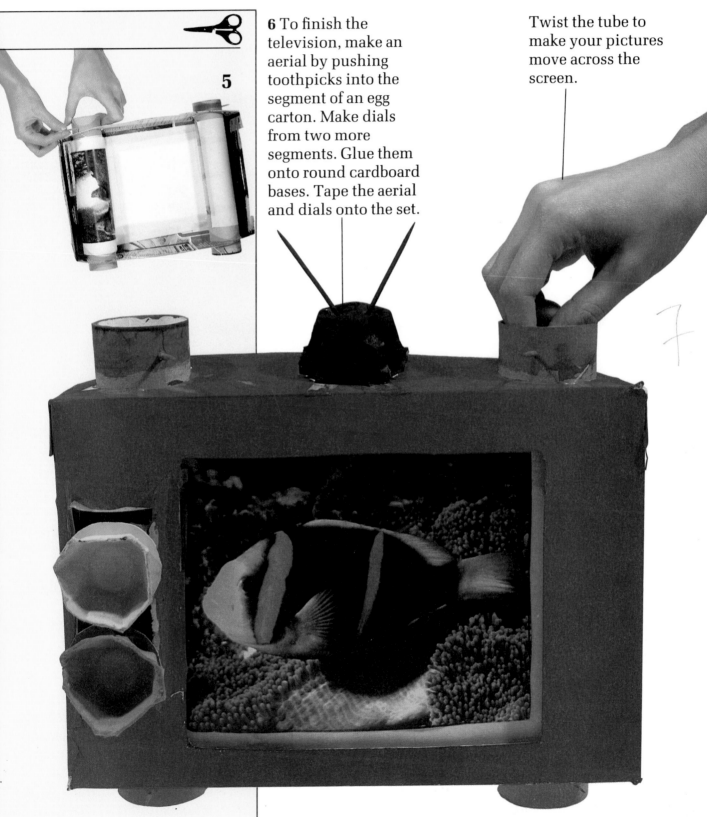

5

6 To finish the television, make an aerial by pushing toothpicks into the segment of an egg carton. Make dials from two more segments. Glue them onto round cardboard bases. Tape the aerial and dials onto the set.

Twist the tube to make your pictures move across the screen.

DRAG RACER

Drag racers or dragsters are cars with very powerful engines that are built to travel as fast as possible. With its streamlined body and impressive exhaust system, your dragster will be ready to win any race.

STEP BY STEP

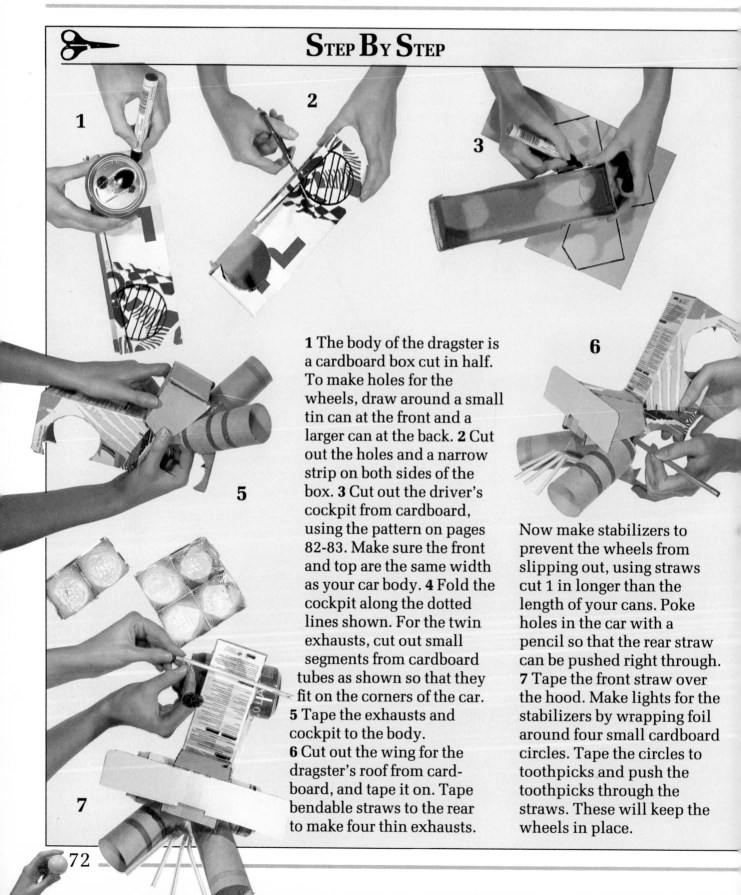

1 The body of the dragster is a cardboard box cut in half. To make holes for the wheels, draw around a small tin can at the front and a larger can at the back. 2 Cut out the holes and a narrow strip on both sides of the box. 3 Cut out the driver's cockpit from cardboard, using the pattern on pages 82-83. Make sure the front and top are the same width as your car body. 4 Fold the cockpit along the dotted lines shown. For the twin exhausts, cut out small segments from cardboard tubes as shown so that they fit on the corners of the car. 5 Tape the exhausts and cockpit to the body. 6 Cut out the wing for the dragster's roof from cardboard, and tape it on. Tape bendable straws to the rear to make four thin exhausts.

Now make stabilizers to prevent the wheels from slipping out, using straws cut 1 in longer than the length of your cans. Poke holes in the car with a pencil so that the rear straw can be pushed right through. 7 Tape the front straw over the hood. Make lights for the stabilizers by wrapping foil around four small cardboard circles. Tape the circles to toothpicks and push the toothpicks through the straws. These will keep the wheels in place.

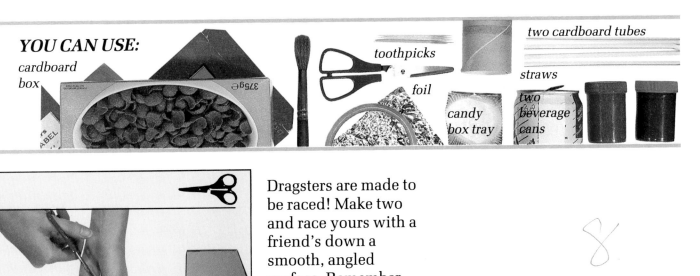

YOU CAN USE:

cardboard box

toothpicks

foil

candy box tray

two beverage cans

two cardboard tubes

straws

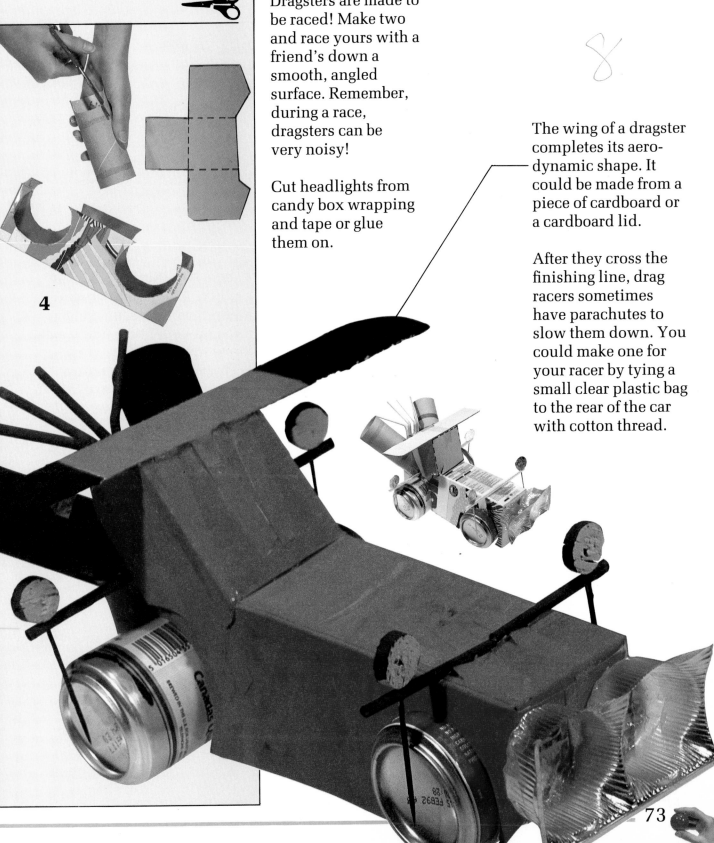

Dragsters are made to be raced! Make two and race yours with a friend's down a smooth, angled surface. Remember, during a race, dragsters can be very noisy!

Cut headlights from candy box wrapping and tape or glue them on.

4

The wing of a dragster completes its aerodynamic shape. It could be made from a piece of cardboard or a cardboard lid.

After they cross the finishing line, drag racers sometimes have parachutes to slow them down. You could make one for your racer by tying a small clear plastic bag to the rear of the car with cotton thread.

73

Biplane With Flying Ace

Biplanes were used by the British, French, and German forces during World War I. With a fearless pilot in the cockpit, this model has a double wing and a propeller that turns as the plane flies through the air.

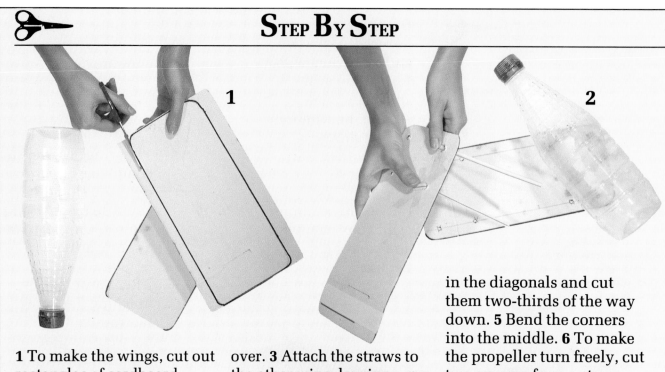

1 To make the wings, cut out rectangles of cardboard, using the pattern on pages 82-83. Make sure the bottle that forms your plane's body fits between the two middle crosses shown on the pattern. Make holes on the crosses. **2** Push drinking straws through the holes in one wing, and bend the ends over. **3** Attach the straws to the other wing, leaving a gap that fits your bottle between the wings. Tape the bottle in place. Cut out cardboard shapes for the tail fin as shown. Fold the top fin and tape it to the crossfin. Tape the fin to the back of the plane. **4** Make the propeller with a square of paper. Mark in the diagonals and cut them two-thirds of the way down. **5** Bend the corners into the middle. **6** To make the propeller turn freely, cut two squares from a straw. Thread one square onto a pin, pin the corners of the propeller to its center, and thread on the other square. **7** Pierce a hole in the bottle top. Put clay inside the top to weight down the plane's nose. Pin the propeller onto the plane.

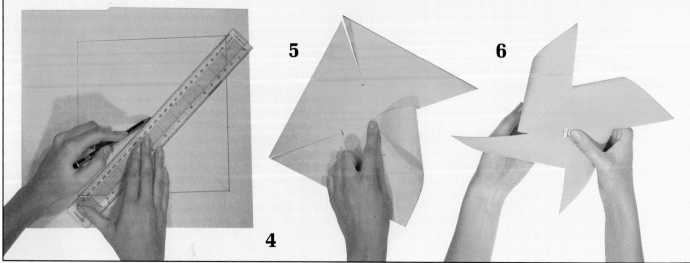

straws

small
yogurt
cup

modeling clay

plastic bottle

pin

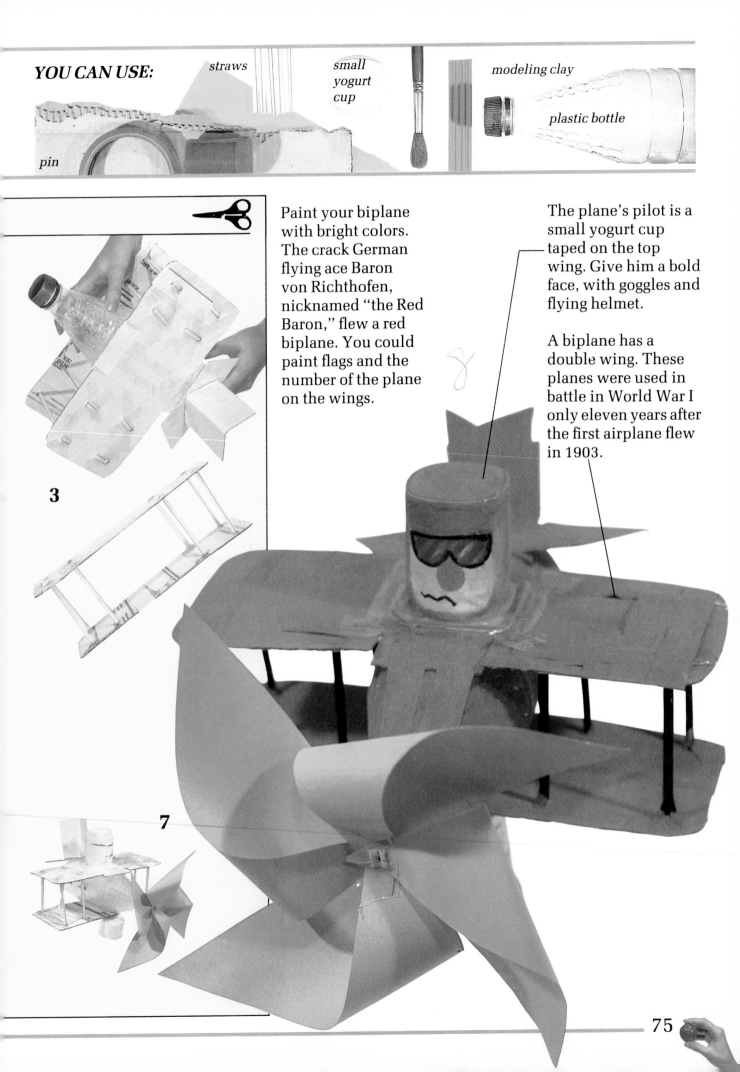

3

Paint your biplane
with bright colors.
The crack German
flying ace Baron
von Richthofen,
nicknamed "the Red
Baron," flew a red
biplane. You could
paint flags and the
number of the plane
on the wings.

The plane's pilot is a
small yogurt cup
taped on the top
wing. Give him a bold
face, with goggles and
flying helmet.

A biplane has a
double wing. These
planes were used in
battle in World War I
only eleven years after
the first airplane flew
in 1903.

7

FLYING THE BIPLANE

Your biplane flies from strings attached to a garden stick control frame. As the plane flies, the propeller spins around. The frame can be held in various positions to make the plane perform different maneuvers.

STEP BY STEP

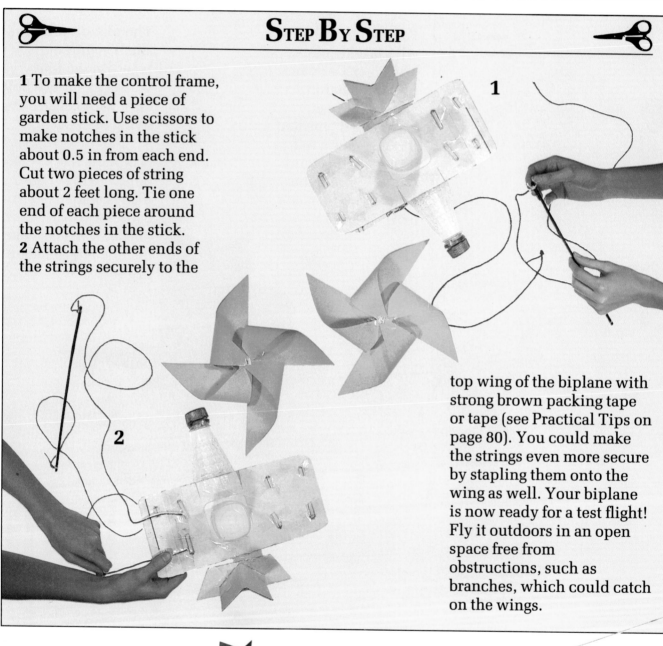

1 To make the control frame, you will need a piece of garden stick. Use scissors to make notches in the stick about 0.5 in from each end. Cut two pieces of string about 2 feet long. Tie one end of each piece around the notches in the stick.
2 Attach the other ends of the strings securely to the

top wing of the biplane with strong brown packing tape or tape (see Practical Tips on page 80). You could make the strings even more secure by stapling them onto the wing as well. Your biplane is now ready for a test flight! Fly it outdoors in an open space free from obstructions, such as branches, which could catch on the wings.

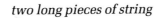

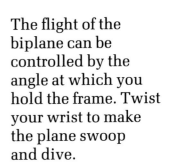

Hold the stick frame with your arm outstretched and the plane dangling down. Swing around in a circle and watch the plane as it lifts off into the air.

The flight of the biplane can be controlled by the angle at which you hold the frame. Twist your wrist to make the plane swoop and dive.

Twist your wrist up to make the biplane ascend. Twist it down to make the plane spiral downward.

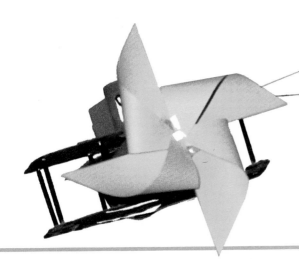

You could also try standing still and whirling the plane above your head like a lasso.

77

MOON BUGGY

This curious vehicle has a powerful dynamo driven by rubber bands. It is designed to carry small extraterrestrials over moon terrain – and over any smooth surface in your home!

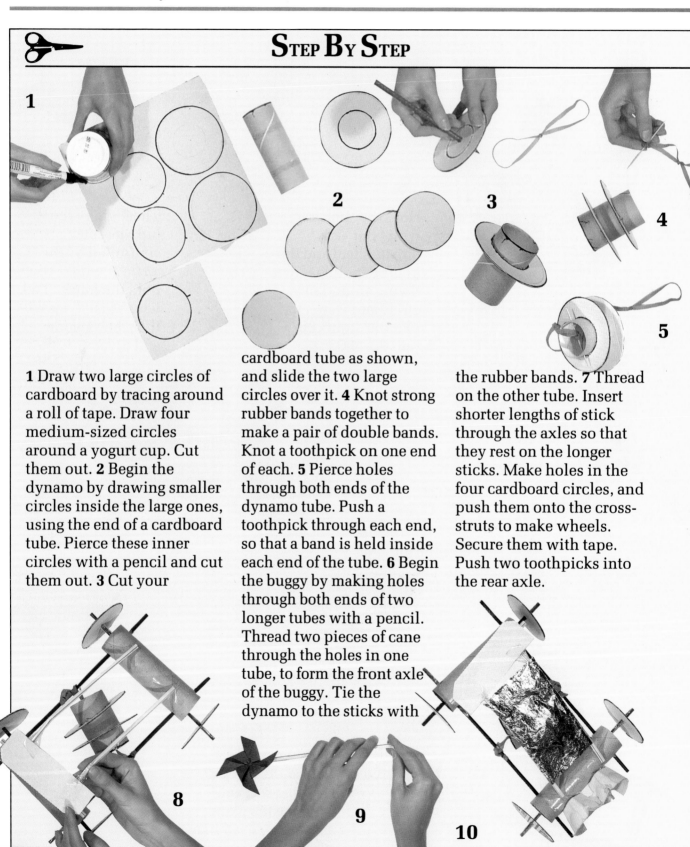

STEP BY STEP

1 Draw two large circles of cardboard by tracing around a roll of tape. Draw four medium-sized circles around a yogurt cup. Cut them out. **2** Begin the dynamo by drawing smaller circles inside the large ones, using the end of a cardboard tube. Pierce these inner circles with a pencil and cut them out. **3** Cut your cardboard tube as shown, and slide the two large circles over it. **4** Knot strong rubber bands together to make a pair of double bands. Knot a toothpick on one end of each. **5** Pierce holes through both ends of the dynamo tube. Push a toothpick through each end, so that a band is held inside each end of the tube. **6** Begin the buggy by making holes through both ends of two longer tubes with a pencil. Thread two pieces of cane through the holes in one tube, to form the front axle of the buggy. Tie the dynamo to the sticks with the rubber bands. **7** Thread on the other tube. Insert shorter lengths of stick through the axles so that they rest on the longer sticks. Make holes in the four cardboard circles, and push them onto the cross-struts to make wheels. Secure them with tape. Push two toothpicks into the rear axle.

YOU CAN USE:

foil

egg carton
cardboard toothpicks

stout cardboard tube

four pieces of garden stick

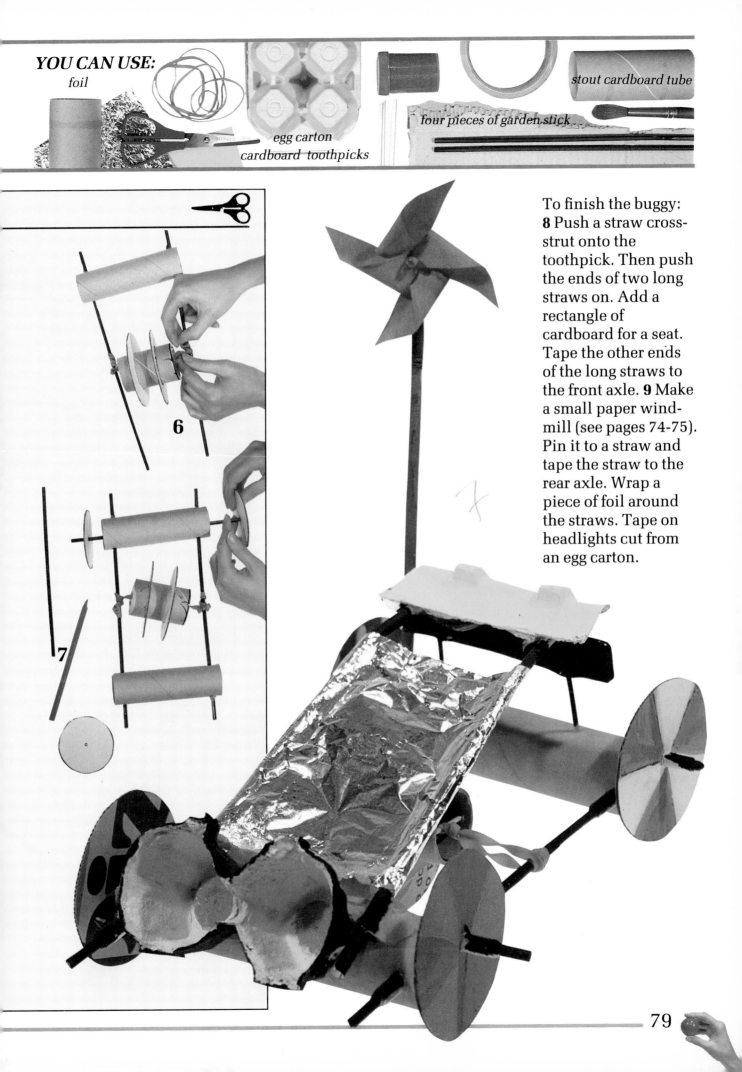

6

7

To finish the buggy:
8 Push a straw cross-strut onto the toothpick. Then push the ends of two long straws on. Add a rectangle of cardboard for a seat. Tape the other ends of the long straws to the front axle. **9** Make a small paper windmill (see pages 74-75). Pin it to a straw and tape the straw to the rear axle. Wrap a piece of foil around the straws. Tape on headlights cut from an egg carton.

PRACTICAL TIPS

Below are a few practical hints that will help you with some of the projects described in this book.

FASTENING
Use this tip for making the biplane (pp 76-77) and whenever you need to fasten string securely.

To fasten thread or string to cardboard, tie a double knot at one end. Place the knot on the cardboard. Lay strips of tape in front of the knot, and press down firmly.

To make your fastening even more secure, you could use packing tape. If you have a stapler, you could staple the knot in place before you tape it down.

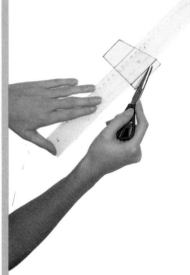

SCORING
Scoring is a way of producing a neat and accurate fold in a piece of paper. You can use this technique to make the rocket's fin, and in other projects, too.

To score paper, place your ruler along the line you want to fold. Press the edge of your scissors lightly along the paper, using the ruler as a guide. Don't press too hard or you may cut through the paper! Then fold along the line you have scored.

PAINTING
It may be difficult to get paint to stick to tape, and to plastic surfaces. If so, this tip will help.

Poster paint has been used to decorate many of the projects in this book. It is usually diluted with water. This paint will stick to plastic if you squirt a little dishwashing liquid into your mixing water. Mix it well before you begin.

RUBBER: rubber bands, balls, balloons, old rubber gloves.

MORE JUNK IDEAS

The materials used most often in this book have been paper, cardboard and plastic packaging. Below are some more suggestions about the kinds of junk that can be used to make and decorate your models.

NATURAL MATERIALS: twigs, leaves, petals, acorns, chestnuts, nuts, pinecones, bark, shells, pebbles, sponge, cork, feathers.

PAPER: newspapers, comics and magazines, postcards and birthday cards, unused wallpaper, tissue.

WOOD: spent matches, garden sticks, cotton spools, lollypop sticks.

FABRIC: yarn, socks, old clothes or sheets, cloth and felt scraps.

PLASTIC: food containers, candy and snack wrappers, buttons, broken toys.

METAL: soft beverage cans, foil, springs, pipe cleaners, hangers, paper clips.

PATTERNS

To use these patterns:
1 Trace the pattern shape onto tracing paper.
2 Turn the tracing over, and place it on top of the paper or cardboard on which you want the image to appear. Scribble over the lines showing through the paper with your pencil. A mirror image of the pattern will appear on the cardboard.

▷ Trace this pattern to make the rocket's fin (see pages 62-63)

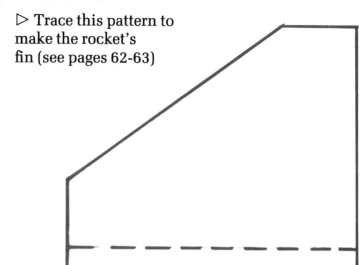

Trace these patterns to
make:
▷ The dragster's roof (see
pages 72-73)

▽ The biplane's wings (see
pages 74-75).

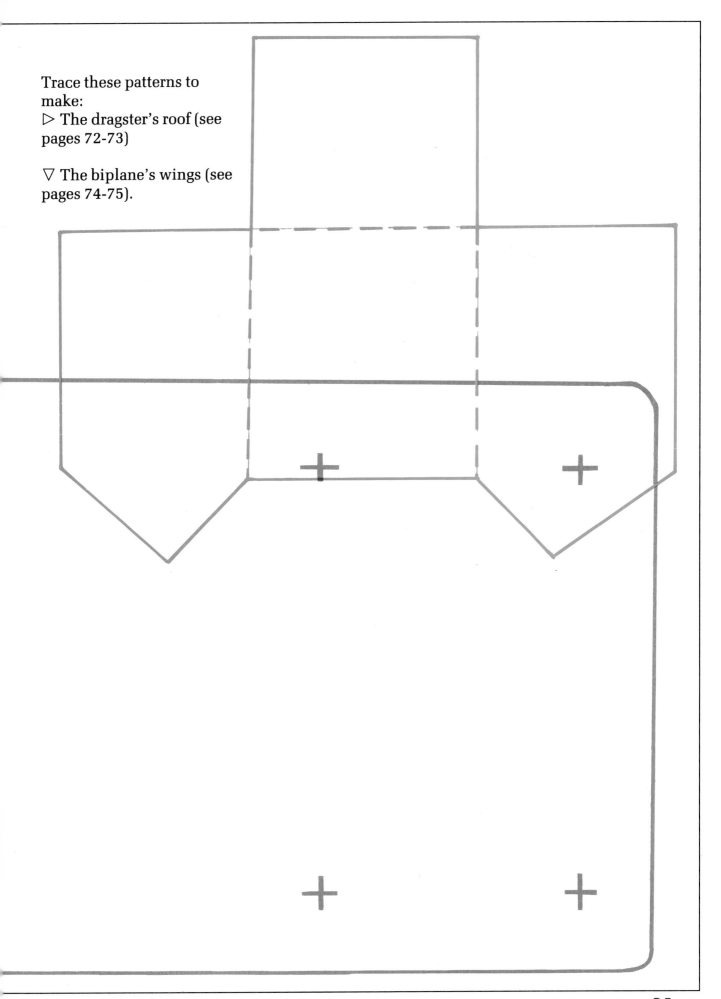

BALLOON-POWERED ROCKET

This simple rocket, driven by a balloon, streaks through space when its balloon is released. The rocket zooms along a string tied between two pieces of furniture.

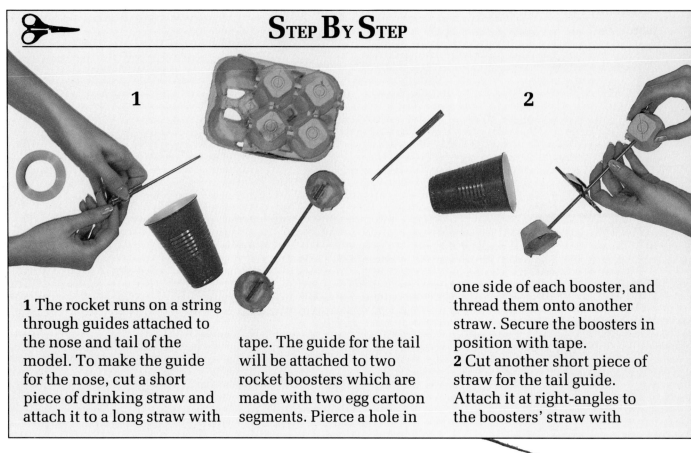

STEP BY STEP

1

2

1 The rocket runs on a string through guides attached to the nose and tail of the model. To make the guide for the nose, cut a short piece of drinking straw and attach it to a long straw with

tape. The guide for the tail will be attached to two rocket boosters which are made with two egg cartoon segments. Pierce a hole in

one side of each booster, and thread them onto another straw. Secure the boosters in position with tape.
2 Cut another short piece of straw for the tail guide. Attach it at right-angles to the boosters' straw with

Your rocket runs along a string anchored between two pieces of furniture. Tie one end of a long piece of string to one anchor point. Thread the other end through the straws on the nose and tail of the rocket. Stretch the string taut and tie it to your second anchor point.

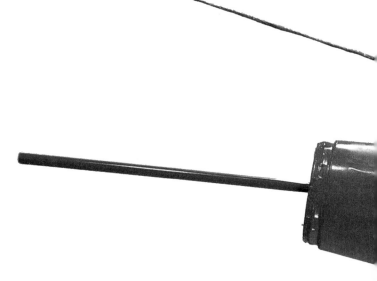

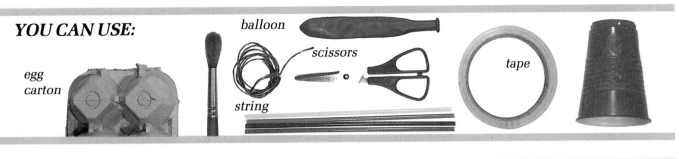

egg
carton

balloon

scissors

string

tape

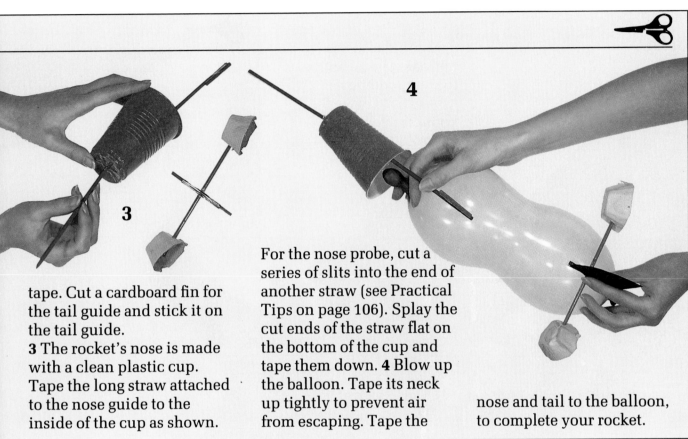

3

4

tape. Cut a cardboard fin for the tail guide and stick it on the tail guide.
3 The rocket's nose is made with a clean plastic cup. Tape the long straw attached to the nose guide to the inside of the cup as shown.

For the nose probe, cut a series of slits into the end of another straw (see Practical Tips on page 106). Splay the cut ends of the straw flat on the bottom of the cup and tape them down. **4** Blow up the balloon. Tape its neck up tightly to prevent air from escaping. Tape the

nose and tail to the balloon, to complete your rocket.

Release the neck of the balloon and watch your rocket jet off along the string!

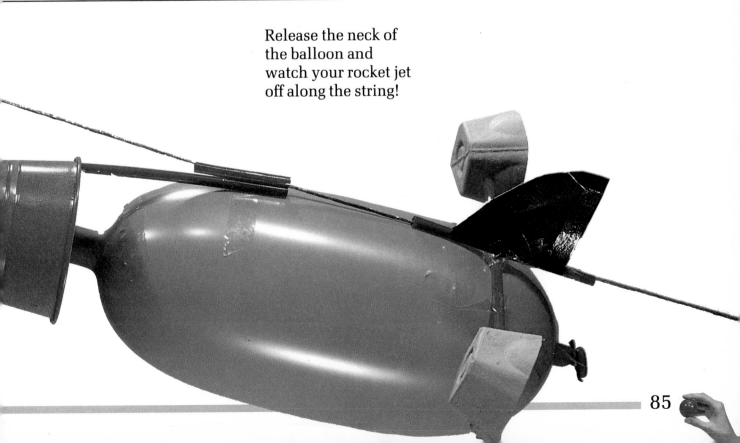

WRIST COMMUNICATOR

No sounds can travel through space, but you can keep in touch with fellow astronauts or with base control with the help of this radio communicator.

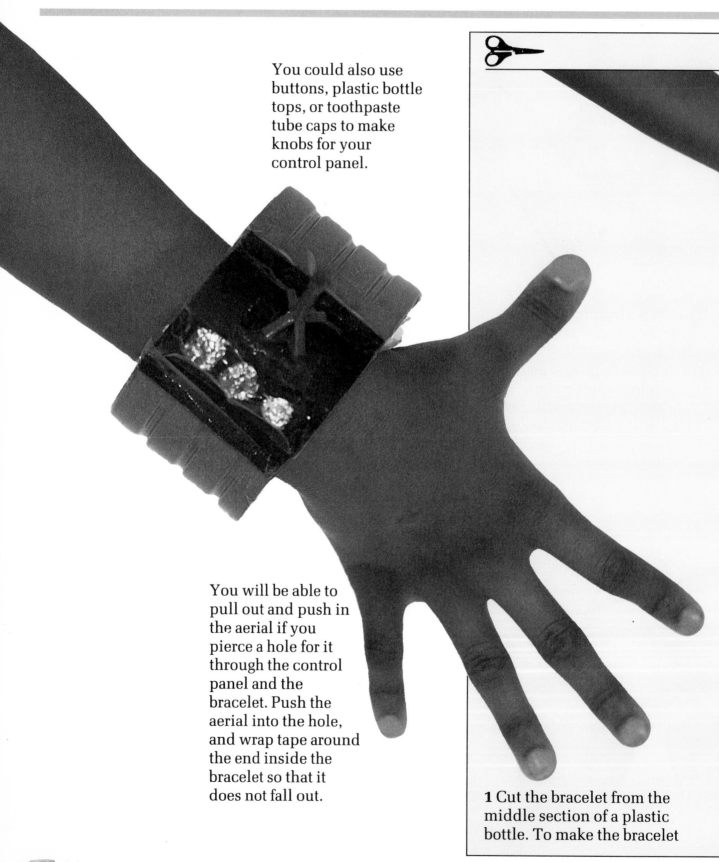

You could also use buttons, plastic bottle tops, or toothpaste tube caps to make knobs for your control panel.

You will be able to pull out and push in the aerial if you pierce a hole for it through the control panel and the bracelet. Push the aerial into the hole, and wrap tape around the end inside the bracelet so that it does not fall out.

1 Cut the bracelet from the middle section of a plastic bottle. To make the bracelet

tinfoil

two toilet paper tubes

drinking straw

plastic bottle

STEP BY STEP

1

2

fit your wrist, you will need adjusters, made from a toilet paper tube. With scissors, cut the tube in half lengthwise and then widthwise, to form four sections. Fold the edges of the sections back to make flaps. Tape the flaps around the inside of the bracelet. Try the bracelet on and add or take away adjusters until it fits. **2** The control panel of

the communicator is made with a quarter section cut from another toilet paper tube. Fold the edges back to make flaps and tape it to the

outside of the bracelet. Now make buttons for the control panel from tinfoil. Roll small pieces of foil into tiny balls and then flatten them between your fingers. Glue or tape them to the panel. Make an antenna for your radio communicator with a drinking straw. Cut a series of slits into one end of the straw. Splay the cut ends of the straw flat onto the panel and tape them down.

ALIEN FEET

These wacky alien feet are a must for space games and fancy dress parties. The ones shown here have long, crinkly veins and brightly colored toes.

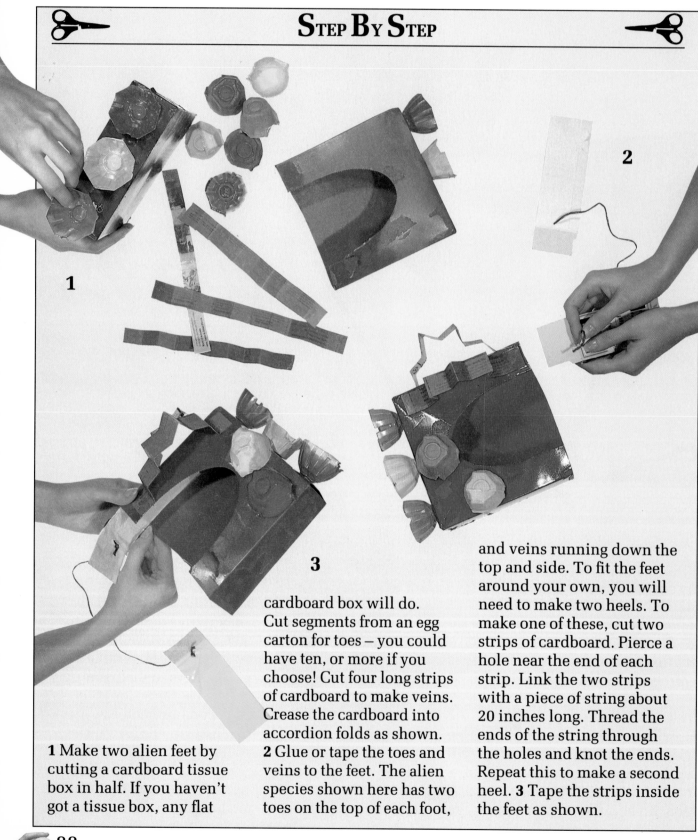

cardboard box will do. Cut segments from an egg carton for toes – you could have ten, or more if you choose! Cut four long strips of cardboard to make veins. Crease the cardboard into accordion folds as shown. **2** Glue or tape the toes and veins to the feet. The alien species shown here has two toes on the top of each foot,

and veins running down the top and side. To fit the feet around your own, you will need to make two heels. To make one of these, cut two strips of cardboard. Pierce a hole near the end of each strip. Link the two strips with a piece of string about 20 inches long. Thread the ends of the string through the holes and knot the ends. Repeat this to make a second heel. **3** Tape the strips inside the feet as shown.

1 Make two alien feet by cutting a cardboard tissue box in half. If you haven't got a tissue box, any flat

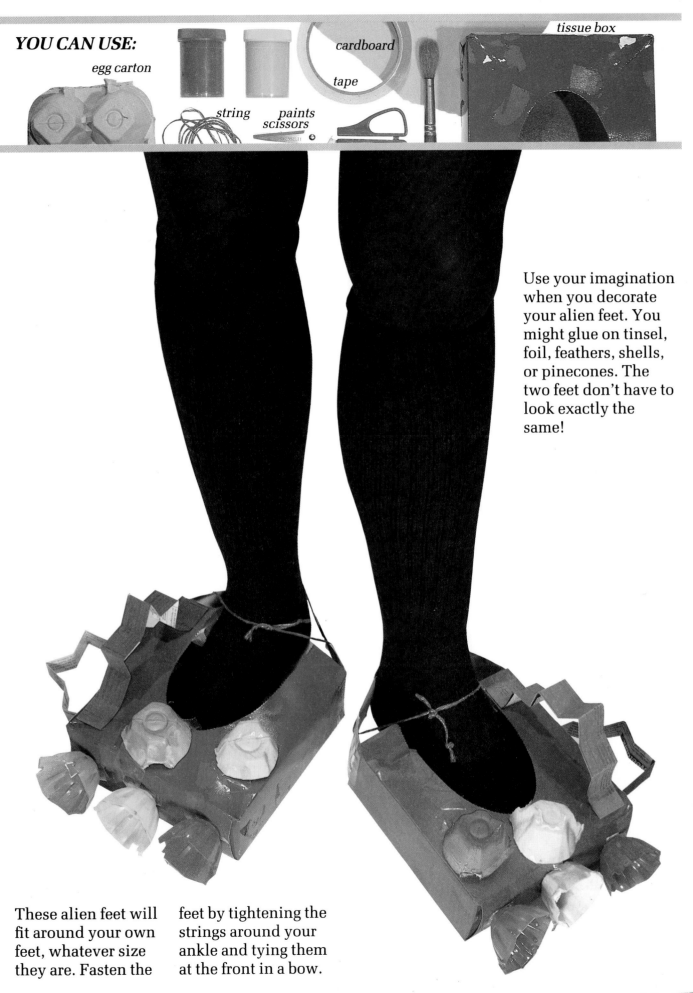

YOU CAN USE:

egg carton

string

paints
scissors

cardboard

tape

tissue box

Use your imagination
when you decorate
your alien feet. You
might glue on tinsel,
foil, feathers, shells,
or pinecones. The
two feet don't have to
look exactly the
same!

These alien feet will
fit around your own
feet, whatever size
they are. Fasten the
feet by tightening the
strings around your
ankle and tying them
at the front in a bow.

89

Reggie The Robot

Reggie is a young robot and his movements can be shy and clumsy. You can control him by using the handle attached to his back.

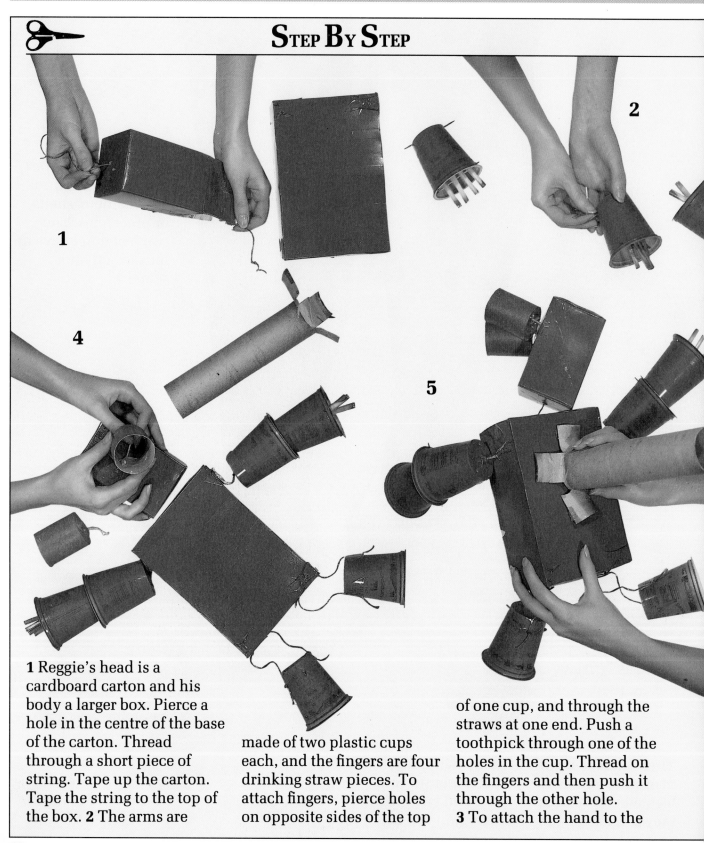

1 Reggie's head is a cardboard carton and his body a larger box. Pierce a hole in the centre of the base of the carton. Thread through a short piece of string. Tape up the carton. Tape the string to the top of the box. **2** The arms are made of two plastic cups each, and the fingers are four drinking straw pieces. To attach fingers, pierce holes on opposite sides of the top of one cup, and through the straws at one end. Push a toothpick through one of the holes in the cup. Thread on the fingers and then push it through the other hole. **3** To attach the hand to the

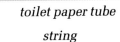

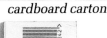

3

tube. Cut slits in one end to make flaps (see page 106).
5 Splay the flaps against

Reggie's back and tape them securely.

arm, pierce holes on opposite sides of the base of the hand cup and top of another cup. Hold the hand cup inside the arm cup, and pass a toothpick through the holes. The hand cup hangs inside the other. To attach an arm to the body, make knots at either end of a piece of string, and tape the string in front of the knots to the arm cup and to the body. **4** Reggie's eyes are made from a toilet paper tube cut in half. Attach them to the head with short pieces of knotted string, as you did the arms. His feet are plastic cups, taped on in the same way. Use longer pieces of string, knotted and taped to both sides of each cup. Now make a control handle for the robot with a paper towel

You can decorate Reggie's chest with a small foil dish, or use bottle and tube tops for knobs and dials.

BUG-EYED MONSTER

This alien species has fearsome eyes that wobble as the monster is pulled along. The model is a fast, smooth runner that can be raced on any flat surface.

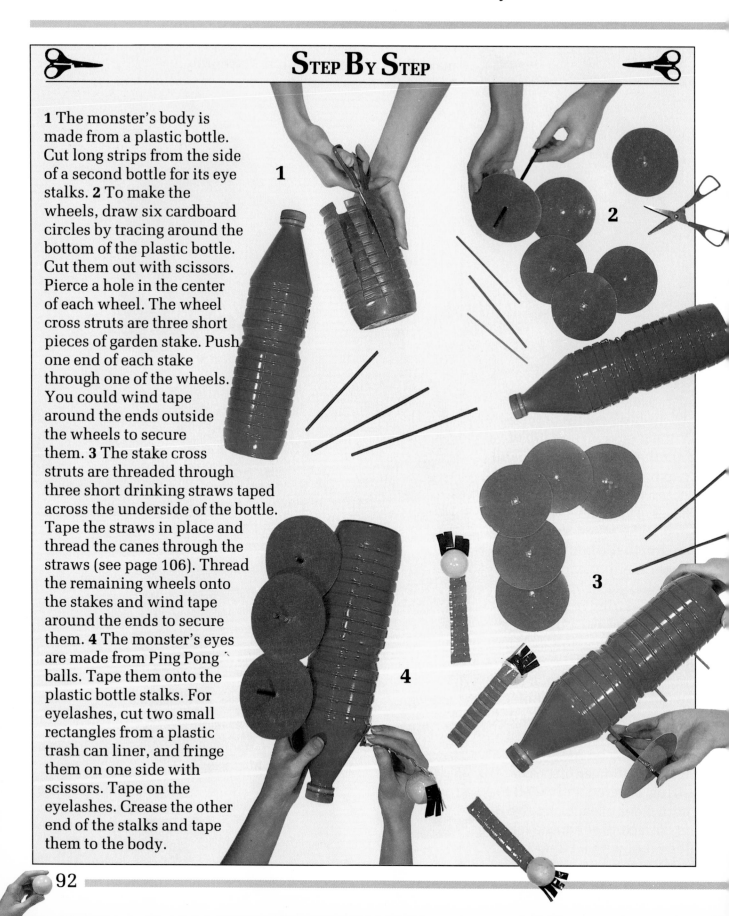

1 The monster's body is made from a plastic bottle. Cut long strips from the side of a second bottle for its eye stalks. **2** To make the wheels, draw six cardboard circles by tracing around the bottom of the plastic bottle. Cut them out with scissors. Pierce a hole in the center of each wheel. The wheel cross struts are three short pieces of garden stake. Push one end of each stake through one of the wheels. You could wind tape around the ends outside the wheels to secure them. **3** The stake cross struts are threaded through three short drinking straws taped across the underside of the bottle. Tape the straws in place and thread the canes through the straws (see page 106). Thread the remaining wheels onto the stakes and wind tape around the ends to secure them. **4** The monster's eyes are made from Ping Pong balls. Tape them onto the plastic bottle stalks. For eyelashes, cut two small rectangles from a plastic trash can liner, and fringe them on one side with scissors. Tape on the eyelashes. Crease the other end of the stalks and tape them to the body.

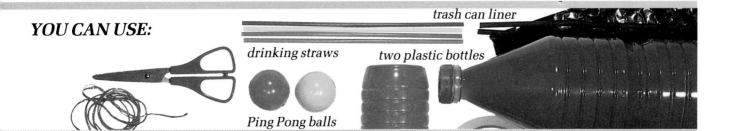

drinking straws

trash can liner

two plastic bottles

Ping Pong balls

Paint your monster with bright poster colors. You could paint the body with spots or stripes.

You could attach a string to the front of the monster's body to pull it along. Or make two models with a friend, and race them down a smooth, angled surface.

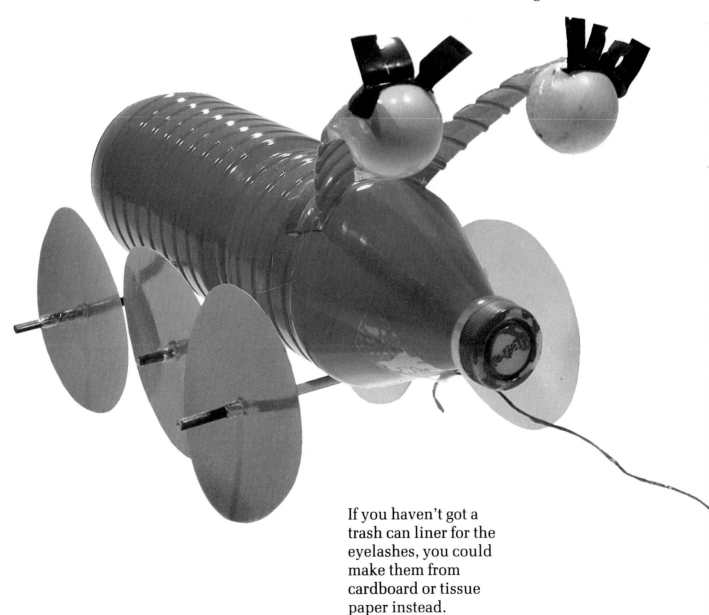

If you haven't got a trash can liner for the eyelashes, you could make them from cardboard or tissue paper instead.

RAY GUN & ZAPPING PISTOL

No star war would be complete without a ray gun or pistol to zap unwary aliens. But beware, the monsters you meet may fight back with weapons of their own!

STEP BY STEP

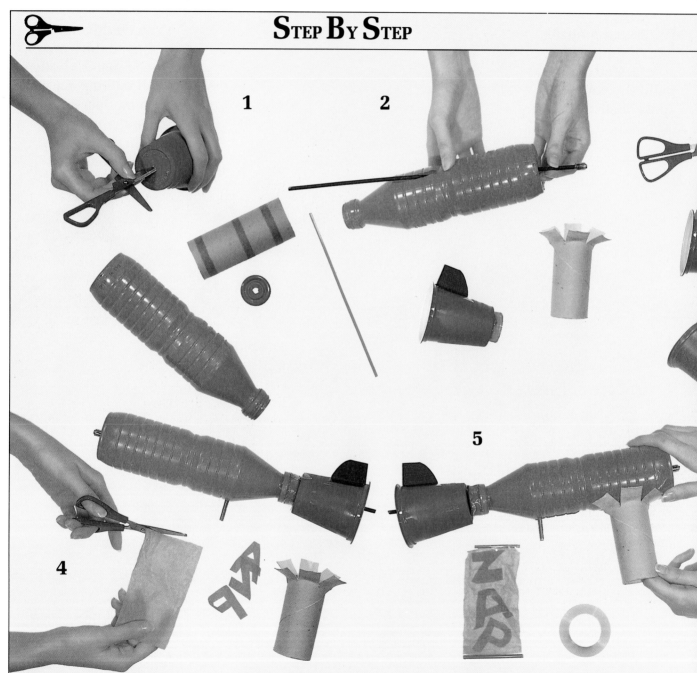

1 For the zapping pistol's barrel and muzzle, pierce a hole through the base of a cup, and through the lid and base of a bottle. **2** For the handle, cut slits into the end of a toilet paper tube. Splay the end flat (see page 106). Cut a fin shape from cardboard and tape it to the muzzle. Cut a trigger slot in the side of the bottle, about 2in long and ½in wide. Wind tape around one end of a garden stake. Push the other end through the bottle's base and the trigger slot. **3** For the trigger, fold a drinking straw in half and tape it around the stake. **4** Push the stake through the neck of the bottle. Thread the bottle top onto the stake and screw it on

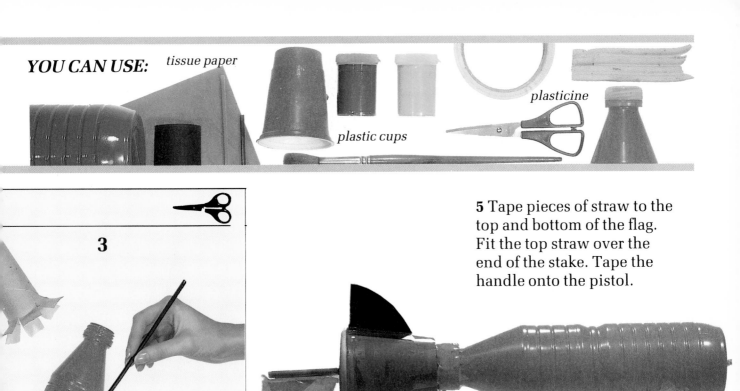

3

6

5 Tape pieces of straw to the top and bottom of the flag. Fit the top straw over the end of the stake. Tape the handle onto the pistol.

To load the pistol, pull the trigger back with your finger. To fire it, push the trigger forward. The flag will pop from the muzzle and unfurl to zap your victim.

the bottle. Thread on the cup. For the Zap! flag use a rectangle of paper. Cut the letters from different colored paper and glue them on.

The ray gun (**6**) is made in the same way as the pistol, but it has no zapping mechanism. You will need a large plastic bottle and another cardboard tube to make a second handle.

95

SPACE VOYAGER MOBILE

This mobile features an astronaut on a trip around our solar system, and some of the sights he or she might expect to see on the way.

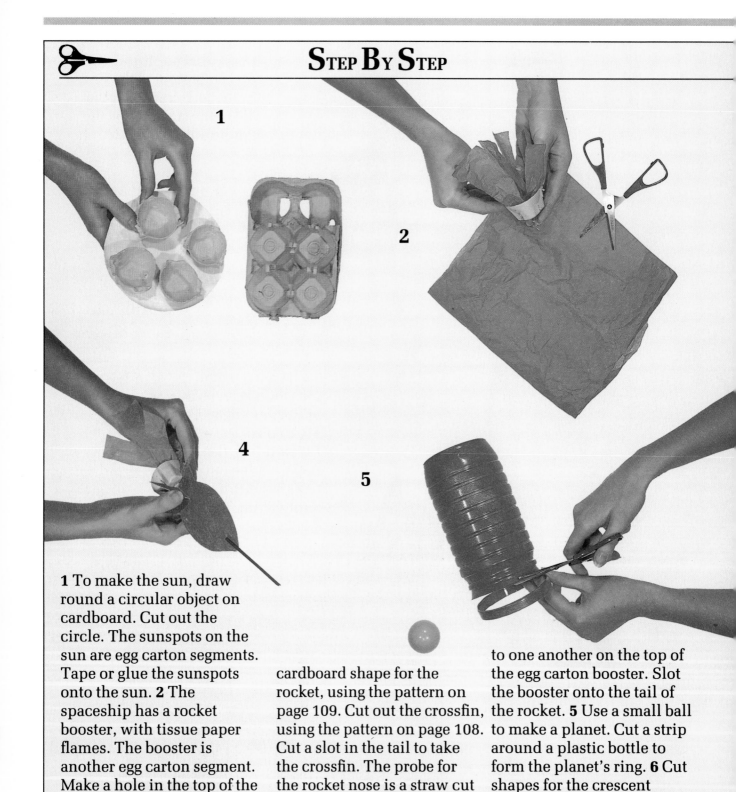

1 To make the sun, draw round a circular object on cardboard. Cut out the circle. The sunspots on the sun are egg carton segments. Tape or glue the sunspots onto the sun. **2** The spaceship has a rocket booster, with tissue paper flames. The booster is another egg carton segment. Make a hole in the top of the booster, and push tissue paper strips through. Secure them with tape. **3** Cut out a cardboard shape for the rocket, using the pattern on page 109. Cut out the crossfin, using the pattern on page 108. Cut a slot in the tail to take the crossfin. The probe for the rocket nose is a straw cut down at an angle as shown. Glue or tape on the probe. **4** Cut four slits at right angles to one another on the top of the egg carton booster. Slot the booster onto the tail of the rocket. **5** Use a small ball to make a planet. Cut a strip around a plastic bottle to form the planet's ring. **6** Cut shapes for the crescent moon and star from cardboard, using the patterns on page 109. Cover them with

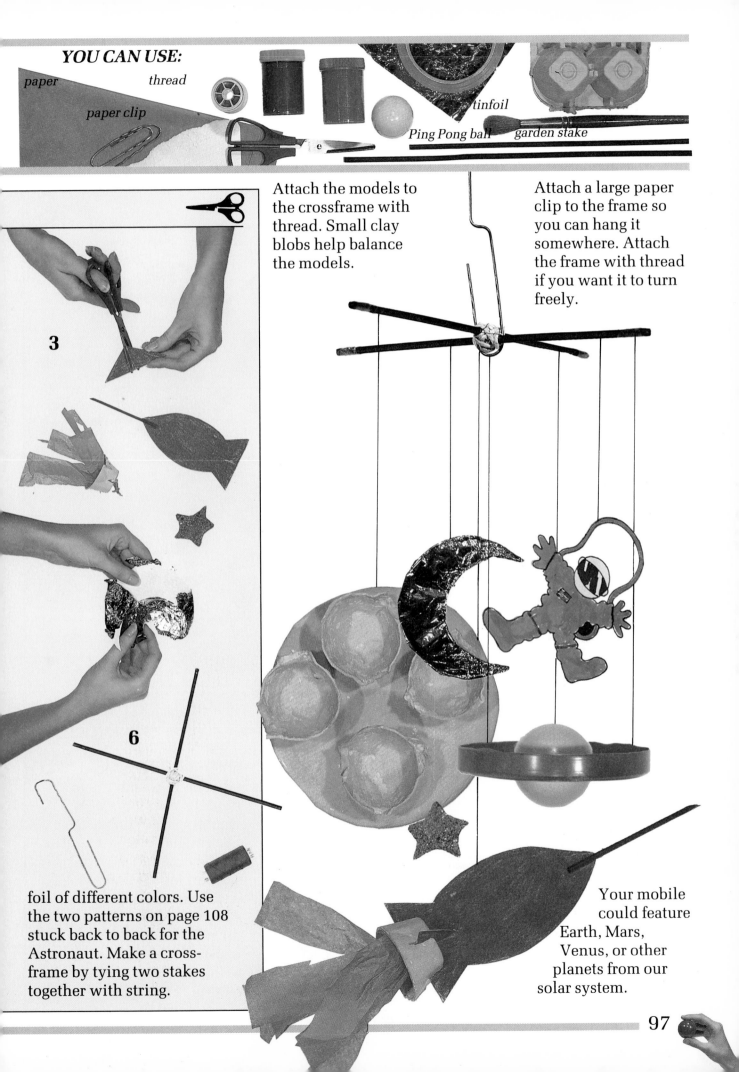

YOU CAN USE:

paper

thread

paper clip

tinfoil

Ping Pong ball   garden stake

Attach the models to the crossframe with thread. Small clay blobs help balance the models.

Attach a large paper clip to the frame so you can hang it somewhere. Attach the frame with thread if you want it to turn freely.

3

6

foil of different colors. Use the two patterns on page 108 stuck back to back for the Astronaut. Make a cross-frame by tying two stakes together with string.

Your mobile could feature Earth, Mars, Venus, or other planets from our solar system.

97

CRAZY MOONBUG

This strange species is adapted to travel in the rough craters of the moon. Its off-center wheels make the model wobble crazily when it is pulled along.

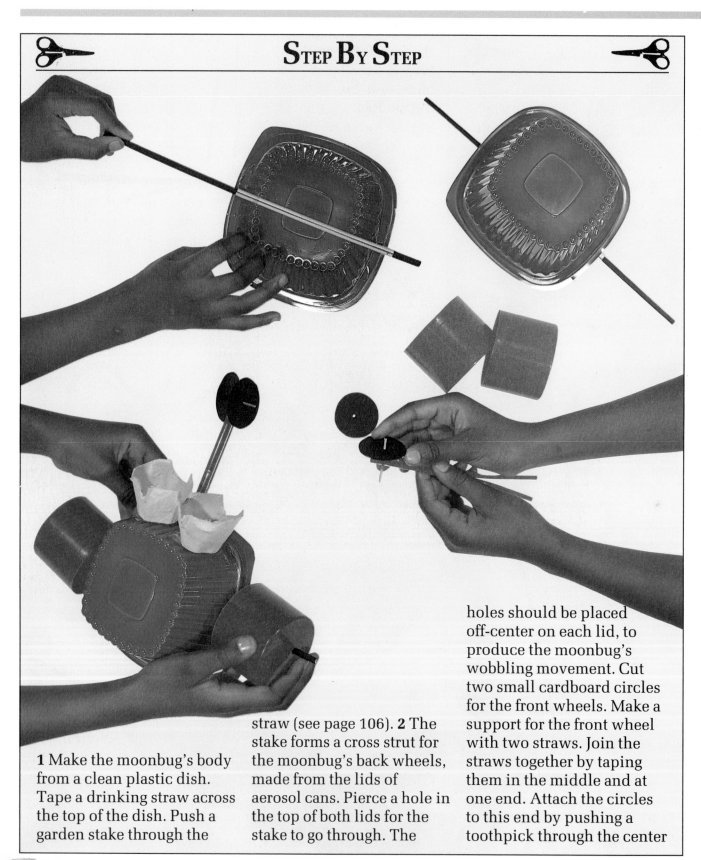

STEP BY STEP

1 Make the moonbug's body from a clean plastic dish. Tape a drinking straw across the top of the dish. Push a garden stake through the straw (see page 106). **2** The stake forms a cross strut for the moonbug's back wheels, made from the lids of aerosol cans. Pierce a hole in the top of both lids for the stake to go through. The holes should be placed off-center on each lid, to produce the moonbug's wobbling movement. Cut two small cardboard circles for the front wheels. Make a support for the front wheel with two straws. Join the straws together by taping them in the middle and at one end. Attach the circles to this end by pushing a toothpick through the center

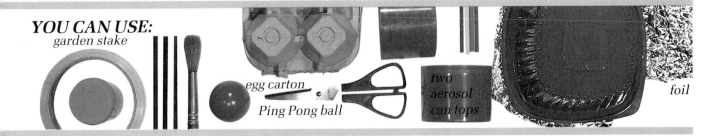

egg carton

Ping Pong ball

two
aerosol
can tops

foil

of one circle, through the straws and then through the other circle. Fold the other ends of the straws back to form a T-shape. **3** Tape the T-shape to the front of the moonbug's body. Push the back wheels onto the cross strut. Cut two egg carton segments for eyes and tape them on.

Tape on a Ping Pong or cotton ball for moonbug's nose. Paint pupils in the egg carton eyes.

Cut strips of tinfoil, yarn, or tissue paper to make hair. Tape or glue them to the moonbug's head.

You could also use a large plastic cup for moonbug's body, and segments cut from a chocolate box tray to make the eyes.

FLYING SAUCER OUTFIT

This spectacular outfit should provide you with a passport to parties and games on planet Earth and throughout the universe.

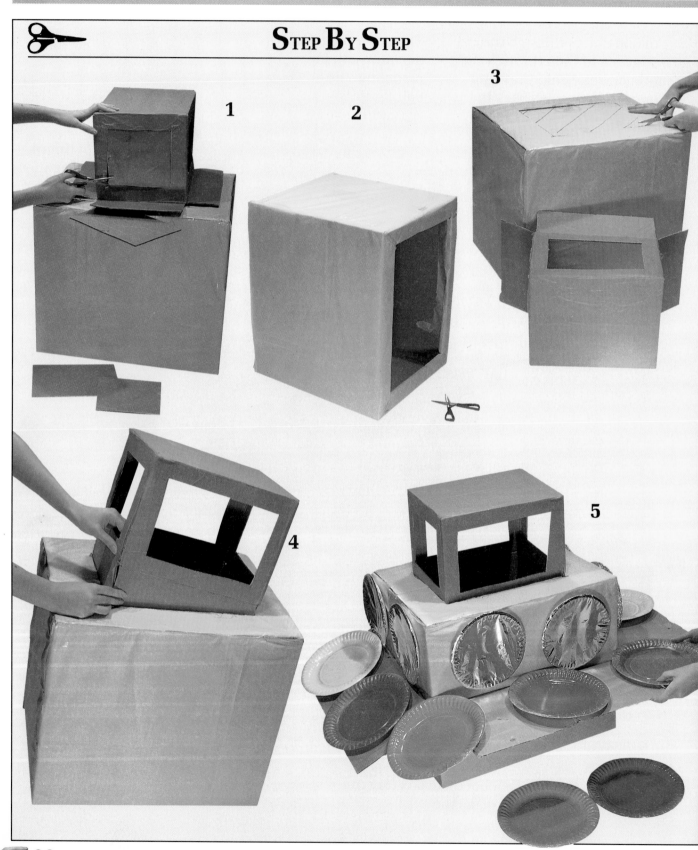

1

2

3

4

5

YOU CAN USE:

plastic bottles

box

drinking straw

foil

paper plates

1 To make the flying saucer outfit you will need a big cardboard box for the body, and a smaller one for the head. Mark a large square inside each of the four sides on the small box. Cut the squares out with scissors. **2** Mark a large square on the bottom of the big box and cut it out. **3** Close the small box and place it on top of the big one. Mark around the small box with a pen and cut out the square that you have drawn on the big box. **4** Open the flaps of the small box and push them through the neck hole you made in the big box.

Tape the flaps of the small box flat inside the top of the big box. **5** Now build the saucer shape around the body, using large flaps of cardboard. Fold the flaps around the body as shown, and tape them on. Tape cardboard struts under the flaps if you want them to stick out. Decorate the saucer shape with cardboard circles or paper plates.

Paint your saucer outfit with bright poster paint. You could wrap tinfoil around some of the cardboard circles on the body. You could also cut armholes in the body if you wish.

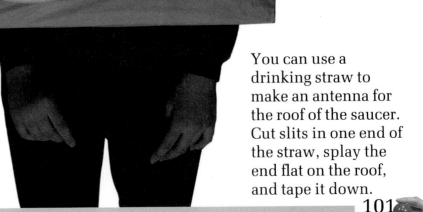

You can use a drinking straw to make an antenna for the roof of the saucer. Cut slits in one end of the straw, splay the end flat on the roof, and tape it down.

101

POWERED SPACE CRAWLER

This small, menacing creature has a generator driven by a rubber band. Wind up the generator, and watch the alien creep along.

STEP BY STEP

1 Make the crawler's body by cutting two strips of trash can liner (or black paper) about 4 x 3 in. Fringe both strips with scissors.
2 Make the crawler's eyes by cutting a small circle of paper in half. Now begin the creature's generator by cutting a piece of candle about ½ in long. Remove the wick from the piece of candle and enlarge the hole a little. Thread a small rubber band through the hole. You may need to hook it through using a bit of wire or a straightened paper clip.
3 Push a toothpick through the loop at one end of the rubber band to secure it inside the candle. Hook the other end through a cotton spool. **4** Fasten a paper clip onto this end of the rubber band and tape the clip firmly to the side of the spool. Now straighten out two paper clips, and tape one along the top of each of the fringes you made earlier. **5** Make one end of each clip into a hook. Push the hooks into the hole in the candle, so that they sit over the toothpick.

YOU CAN USE:

rubber bands

trash can liner

cotton spool

candle

paper

toothpick

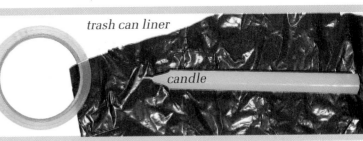

3

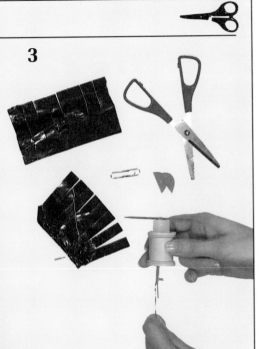

6

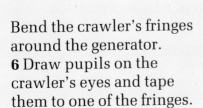

Bend the crawler's fringes around the generator.
6 Draw pupils on the crawler's eyes and tape them to one of the fringes.

To wind up the crawler's generator, hold the candle and toothpicks firmly in one hand and turn the cotton spool with the other hand. Give the spool a number of turns. Put the crawler down on a flat surface and watch it as it creeps along.

The crawler's toothpick should lift the creature up over objects placed in its path.

Make a different species of alien by using tinfoil instead of a trash can liner to make the body.

Pop-up Moonscape

Surprise your friends with this cratered moonscape, apparently devoid of life.
Place the box on a flat surface, and watch three aliens shoot from the craters!

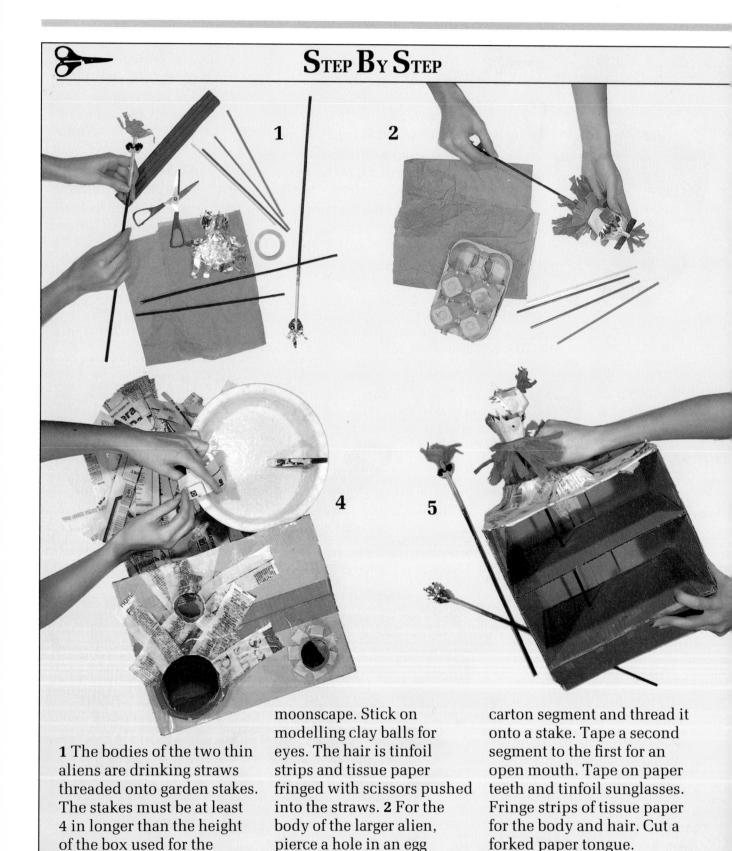

Step By Step

1 The bodies of the two thin aliens are drinking straws threaded onto garden stakes. The stakes must be at least 4 in longer than the height of the box used for the moonscape. Stick on modelling clay balls for eyes. The hair is tinfoil strips and tissue paper fringed with scissors pushed into the straws. **2** For the body of the larger alien, pierce a hole in an egg carton segment and thread it onto a stake. Tape a second segment to the first for an open mouth. Tape on paper teeth and tinfoil sunglasses. Fringe strips of tissue paper for the body and hair. Cut a forked paper tongue.

YOU CAN USE:

cardboard box
newspaper

toilet paper tube

flour and
water paste

egg carton

plastic bottle

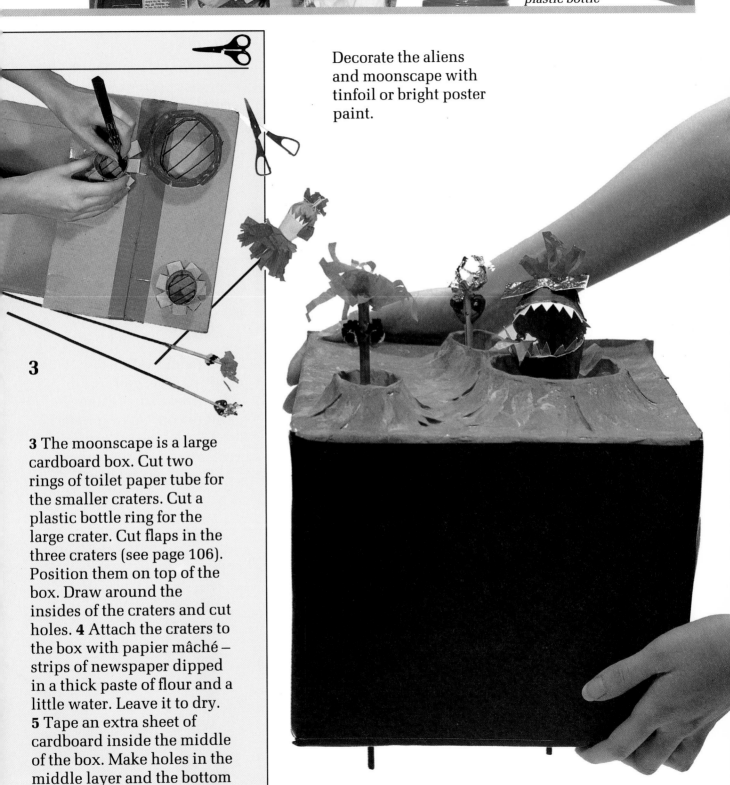

Decorate the aliens
and moonscape with
tinfoil or bright poster
paint.

3

3 The moonscape is a large
cardboard box. Cut two
rings of toilet paper tube for
the smaller craters. Cut a
plastic bottle ring for the
large crater. Cut flaps in the
three craters (see page 106).
Position them on top of the
box. Draw around the
insides of the craters and cut
holes. **4** Attach the craters to
the box with papier mâché –
strips of newspaper dipped
in a thick paste of flour and a
little water. Leave it to dry.
5 Tape an extra sheet of
cardboard inside the middle
of the box. Make holes in the
middle layer and the bottom
of the box below the craters.
Thread the stakes through
the holes. Tape the box shut.

PRACTICAL TIPS

Below are a few practical hints to help you with some of the projects described in this book and with your model-making in general.

MAKING WHEELS

This tip will help you with all models that run on wheels, such as the moonbug on pages 98-99.

Whether your wheels are made of cardboard or plastic, they will need a cross strut or axle on which they can rotate freely. A stake pushed through a drinking straw makes a good axle. If you want your model to bounce along, as the moonbug does, pierce holes for the axle off-center of your wheels.

Push the wheels onto the axle. Wind a little tape around the stake outside the wheel to secure it.

CREATING FLAPS

Use this tip for the projects on pages 86-87, 94-95, 100-101, and 104-105, and for fastening tube shapes on your models in general.

Cut a number of short slits around one end of the tube with scissors. The slits create a series of flaps. Bend

the flaps outward. Now you will be able to press the tube flat onto the surface of your model. Attach the tube to the model with glue, tape or papier mâché.

PAINTING

Poster paint, diluted with water, has been used to decorate many of the projects in this book.

To get paint to stick to plastic or tape, you could add a little dishwashing liquid to your mixing water. Stir it round with your brush or with a stick to mix it well before you begin.

NATURAL MATERIALS:
twigs, leaves, petals, acorns, chestnuts, nuts, pinecones, bark, shells, pebbles, sponge, cork, feathers.

MORE JUNK IDEAS

The materials used most often in this book have been paper, cardboard and plastic packaging. Below are some more suggestions about the kinds of junk that can be used to make and decorate your models.

PAPER: newspapers, comics and magazines, postcards and birthday cards, unused wallpaper, tissue.

WOOD: garden stakes, clothespegs, cotton spools, lolly sticks.

PLASTIC: food containers, sweet and crisp wrappers, buttons, broken toys.

FABRIC: wool, socks, old clothes or sheets, cloth, and felt scraps.

METAL: soft drink cans, tin foil, springs, pipecleaners, coathangers, paper clips.

PATTERNS

These patterns are for you to trace to help you with some of the models made in this book. You can create your own patterns very easily.

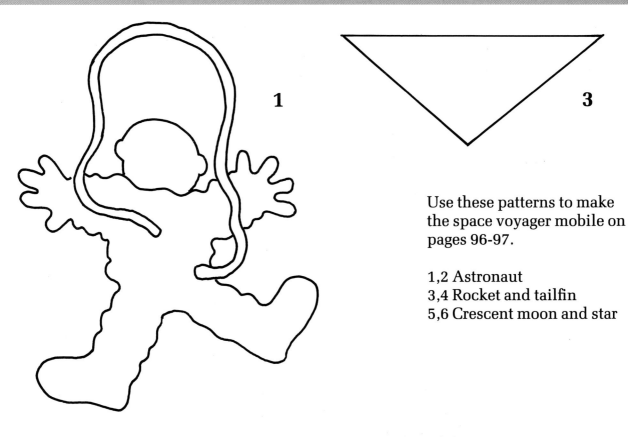

1

3

Use these patterns to make the space voyager mobile on pages 96-97.

1,2 Astronaut
3,4 Rocket and tailfin
5,6 Crescent moon and star

To use these patterns:
1 Trace the pattern shape onto tracing paper or thin bond paper.
2 Turn the tracing over, and place it on top of the paper or cardboard on which you want the image to appear. Scribble over the lines showing through the paper with your pencil. A mirror image of the pattern will appear on the cardboard.

2

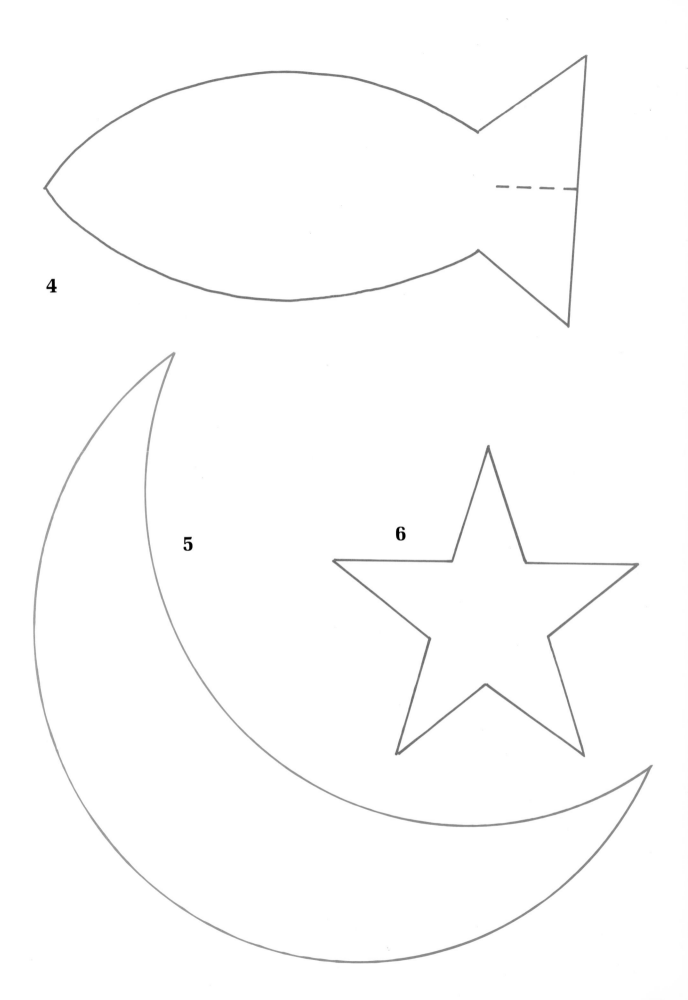

4

5

6

INDEX